Edited by Ian Latham
Concept by Ian Latham and Mark Swenarton

Copyright © 2011 Right Angle Publishing Ltd
All rights reserved. No part of this publication may be reproduced in any manner whatsoever without prior permission in writing from Right Angle Publishing.

First published by Right Angle Publishing
161 Rosebery Avenue, London EC1R 4QX

British Library Cataloguing in Publication Data
A catalogue record for this book is available from the British Library

ISBN 0 9532848 3 2
ISBN-13: 978-0-9532848-3-2

ALLIES AND MORRISON

Edited by Ian Latham with essays by Richard MacCormac and Robert Tavernor

Contents

8	**Ideals and Circumstances** Richard MacCormac		
10	**Constructing the City over Time** Robert Tavernor		

19	**Projects 1983–2003**		
20	The Mound	138	Tate Britain Landscape
24	Aston Triangle	142	Horniman Museum
26	The Clove Building	148	Michael Horniman Conservation Building
30	Felsted School	150	South Hill Park Arts Centre
32	Sainsbury's Supermarket	154	The Hospital
34	British Museum Forecourt	156	St Martin's Court, Paternoster Square
36	Centrepoint Windshelf	158	Holden House
38	Minories	160	Blackburn House
40	Dulwich Picture Gallery	164	Blackwell
44	Scott Howard Building	168	6 Brindleyplace
46	University of Essex Library	170	Scotch Malt Whisky Society
50	Oak Yard	172	Cowdray Park Golf Club
54	Stephen Bull's Bistro and Bar	174	Fulham Broadway
58	Admiral Court, Blandford Street	178	Milton Keynes College
62	National Museum of Contemporary Art, Helsinki	182	Newnham College Library
66	People's Palace, Royal Festival Hall	184	The Guardian and Observer Archive
70	South Bank Centre Temporary Installations	188	One Piccadilly Gardens
72	South Bank Masterplan	192	London College of Communication
76	Sarum Hall School	196	John Makepeace Workshop
82	Liverpool Pierhead	198	Queen's House
86	British Embassy, Dublin		
94	Nunnery Square		
98	Rosalind Franklin Building, Newnham College		
106	Students' Union Shop, University of Southampton		
108	Regent Street Masterplan	201	**Appendices**
110	Contemporary Applied Arts		
114	Abbey Mills Pumping Station	202	Chronology
122	Prince of Wales Road	210	Bibliography
128	Rutherford Information Services Building	214	Exhibitions
134	The Place	215	Team

IDEALS AND CIRCUMSTANCES
Richard MacCormac

My first encounter with the architecture of Bob Allies and Graham Morrison was as one of the assessors of The Mound competition in Edinburgh which they won in 1983, a year before their practice was formally established. A subtle understanding of existing levels and layered flights of steps in their proposal brought Playfair's two great asymmetrically placed temples, the Royal Scottish Academy and the National Gallery, into a coherent relationship with one another. Here already evident was a fundamental principle in Allies and Morrison's work, the resolution of the tension between the ideal and the circumstantial, the implicit issue in the uneasy adjacency of Playfair's buildings. With hindsight one can discern in this project other commitments which have subsequently enabled these architects to stake out their position, absorbing the technical virtuosity of mainstream British modernism and making it less self-referential and culturally more allusive. The Mound competition showed them at ease with history and with the idea of composition – and alert to the realisation that it is the relationship between buildings and sites which makes each intelligible.

The next project to attract my attention was the Dulwich Picture Gallery competition, in which Allies and Morrison were placed second. Their design addressed itself to the setting of Soane's masterpiece by reaffirming the building line set up by the almshouses to the north. There was a sense that the site had been layered, the linearity of their proposal reinforcing the longitudinal character of Soane's gallery, which became the backdrop to a newly-formed court. The external wall of the multipurpose hall was allowed to take up the alignment of College Road, setting up a discordant element which, as Aalto showed, can sharpen the appetite for order itself.

The idea of layering continued throughout the plan and its organisation, a reminder of the Soane Museum in Lincoln's Inn Fields. It was reinforced by a central top-lit circulation spine which ran north-south providing access to all public spaces. The elevations also consisted of a sequence of layers – structure, glazed openings, sliding security shutters and brise-soleils – all combined with the serendipity we associate with traditional Japanese architecture but mediated in materials and detail by a Scandinavian sensibility. Here already were the ingredients and tactics of the practice's mature work.

It is always tempting to try to classify the output of an architectural practice, to provide a critical framework for evaluating each project. One might say that one end of the spectrum of work is marked by the formal urban project which addresses the city around it; and the other is marked by house-like (or barn-like) pavilions with more rural or suburban connotations. The former would include masterplans and projects for public buildings and offices, most of which have not been realised – Royal Victoria Docks (1988), masterplan for the South Bank (1994), offices in Botolph Lane (1993) and the Regent Street masterplan (1995) among them. The architecture of these urban projects has a classical resonance with the traditional hierarchies of scale distilled into a modern vocabulary. The house-like or barn-like projects on the other hand are usually independent buildings in their own setting, with pitched roofs and bricks and timber used in addition or in counterpoint to steel, glass and stone. These projects include Graham Morrison's own house (1989-92), Sarum Hall School (1995), Newnham College (1995), the Dublin Embassy (1995) and Abbey Mills Pumping Station (1997).

This distinction may be a useful approximation and a recognition in the work of the duality of two inherited traditions: the abstract rectilinear preoccupations of the modern movement in the context of the city and the adaptable English arts and crafts tradition applied in more domestic situations. Yet this typological classification does not include a further category in the practice's work – the conversion – a kind of architectural problem which essentially contrasts and reconciles the circumstantial with imposed order. If this is a fundamental characteristic of Allies and Morrison's work then their 1994 proposal for the South Bank may be seen as a key project. The judicious conservation and alteration of the Hayward Gallery and Queen Elizabeth Hall anticipated the approach of the subsequent (2000) Rick Mather masterplan and should surely have made it the winner, rather than the second-placed entry, in 1994. It created an envelope around the existing buildings, externalising foyers and circulation in the manner of the Royal Festival Hall. The consequence was an interaction between the existing buildings, which remained visible, and the surrounding structures of a renewed urban order. This tension between the aspiration towards order and the accommodation of disorder distinguishes the architecture of Allies and Morrison from the reductive orderliness sought both by the modern movement and its British 'high tech' inheritors and by the institutions of modern society. In this regard Graham Morrison refers to the argument of Richard Sennett's book The Uses of Disorder – that the ideal of total orderliness may indicate an unwillingness to face conflict and that allowing for the possibility of disorder may result in an altogether more responsive and creative outcome. Interestingly, this possibility for architecture was implicit in the essay 'Order, Orthodoxy and the Orders' written by Bob Allies in 1983. This analysed the facades of Giulio Romano's Palazzo Te in the light of the discovery that the building was not new, but was a conversion which sought to reconcile contradictions between existing structures and new facades. Allies argued that the 'constraints imposed by the existing building acted as powerful stimuli, crucial to the operation of Giulio's creative imagination' and that 'in an extraordinary inversion of the conventional logic… Giulio recognised that the classical language might also offer a means of accommodating disorder in an existing plan… (and) an organisational framework powerful enough to carry all manner of variation'.[1]

Among Allies and Morrison's many highly sophisticated projects the building that I find the most complex and exemplary demonstration of these insights is the British Embassy in Dublin. The pristine formality of the stone facade is eroded to reveal and accommodate another order of metal construction and imply a subordinate inner pre-existing building. This reading is in turn overlaid by the effect of the embedded metal grid which slices through the stonework and extends beyond it, so that the stone itself becomes subordinate. Typologically the project seems to combine the formality of the urban projects with the informality of the house-like buildings. The diplomatic propriety of the formal front facade conceals a courtyard where brickwork appearing from behind layers of stone again suggests pre-existing out-buildings.

The work of Allies and Morrison sustains a position which contrasts sharply with the exuberant irrationality of currently fashionable architects whose work emerged as a riposte to the emptiness of commercial modernism. But to me their work seems to offer a more real prospect for the future because it has developed a language that manages to be both ordinary and yet very subtle, to reconcile the ideal with the pragmatic and combine a historical sense with the surprises of real creativity.

1 'Order, Orthodoxy and the Orders', Bob Allies, Architectural Review, pp59-65, June 1983.

British Embassy, Dublin, 1995

CONSTRUCTING THE CITY OVER TIME
Robert Tavernor

The architecture of Bob Allies and Graham Morrison is in many ways antithetical to the exaggerated, individual rhetoric of much contemporary architecture. It does not sit comfortably alongside an avant-garde fascination for consumerism and hyper-technology. Nor, compared to the spatial and visual extravagances of modern Neo-Baroque is their architecture exuberant. Rather than being eye-catching and exciting comment, their buildings are meticulous in their politeness. They do not design buildings that are isolated statements, physically or culturally. Their buildings are purposively designed to look as if they have always been an essential and complementary part of the existing urban landscape.[1]

This is not a straightforward starting-point but it is where their value lies. Their architecture is born out of a hard-won understanding of the formal and social evolution of the European city. They are cultured urbanists, and their profound knowledge of the historic and modern city has enabled them to extend – through interpretation and invention – the thread of normality and convention that connects the diversity of western architecture. Appreciating the value in what is normal and conventional, they excel and delight in being 'ordinary' and 'without rhetoric' – a peculiarly English response to modern architecture.[2] Unlike recent manifestations of this aesthetic,[3] however, the traditional notion of figurative elegance, involving proportion and refinement, is a priority in their work.

Their architectural direction was set by the decade in which they studied. Graham Morrison graduated from the University of Cambridge in 1975 and Bob Allies from Edinburgh in 1977. Architecture students in 1970s Britain were very conscious that they were living in a time of transition. The enlightened social idealism of democracy that had shaped modernism at birth, and that had been eagerly assimilated by post-war British politicians and celebrated during the 1960s, appeared during the 70s to have been corrupted irrevocably by politicians and developers. Modernism was variously described as moribund, dying, or already dead. For students there appeared to be two extreme routes through the turmoil of those years: to go with the flow and be swept into an uncertain future; or to search out handholds in the fundamental values of the past. Bob Allies and Graham Morrison chose the latter. They sought a quiet unassuming stability for their architecture, a centre in and around which the flux of modern life could be measured, understood and enjoyed. They based their inquiry on study and the first-hand experience of the European city.

They both cite Aldo Rossi's, The Architecture of the City (first published in Italian in 1966), and Robert Venturi's Complexity and Contradiction in Architecture (published in America in the same year), as crucial to their approach.[4] Arguably the first major reassessment of the modern movement, these two books provided an eloquent critique of the functionalism that characterised the post-war era. Rossi attacked what he saw as the neglect and destruction of the traditional (European) city – which he regarded as the container and representation of 'the collective memory' – and argued for the restoration of the craft of architecture and the reinstatement of the public realm. Venturi focused on architectural form and the sterility of modern buildings brought about by the modernist rejection of stylistic imagery. He argued for ambiguity of meaning: for buildings with facades and forms that performed a role within the street regardless of their internal programme; and for external walls that differed from those surrounding interior spaces. He maintained that buildings should not strive for a simplistic resolution of their many internal and external relations but instead should express their 'obligation toward the difficult whole'.

Both books had a profound effect on architectural debate, countering the tabula rasa mentality of modernist architect-planners inspired by Le Corbusier. Historical precedent was now seen as an exemplar – particularly the buildings and cities of Italy. Rossi was steeped in Italian history and Venturi also knew Italy well, having been architect in residence at the American Academy in Rome – although he also applauded architects elsewhere, from Lutyens to Aalto.

Keen observation of the historic and recent past is important for Allies and Morrison. It provides a source for speculation on the future and they have explicitly acknowledged the influence in their work of key moments in the last five hundred years of architectural tradition. They succeeded in sidestepping the postmodern stylistic frenzy that greeted Venturi's manifesto by going beyond the text, and making first-hand studies of the past. Morrison, while still at Cambridge – a school that under the leadership of Leslie Martin and Colin St John Wilson had a particular affinity with Scandinavian modernism – went to Finland in 1972, to work in the office of Keijo Petäjä. His direct experience of Aalto's architecture was decisive in the aesthetic he would later develop. Allies won the Rome Scholarship in 1981. During his nine-month residence in Rome, he studied the architecture of the sixteenth and seventeenth centuries, including Giulio Romano and Bernini, and on his return published a study of Giulio Romano's Palazzo Te in Mantua. His comprehension of this project, where Giulio Romano created something powerfully new from the buildings that pre-existed on that site, proved decisive for Allies's own development as an architect.[5] The potential of urban transformation particularly excited him. Rome fascinated Allies as a palimpsest – not the horizontal layering of building-on-building whereby the pre-existing is erased, but the three-dimensional transformations that are visible above ground, whereby buildings assimilate and conjoin new with old. Here was evidence of a visually rich environment in which buildings are not destroyed and begun anew unnecessarily, but are adapted and adjusted to meet changing needs over time.

This reading of Rome was encouraged by the recent publication of Roma Interrotta (1979), a paper design exercise led by Michael Graves involving interventions by a number of international architects in Nolli's 1748 figure-ground plan of Rome.[6] Nolli's plan connects interior space – church interiors and the domestic courtyards of palazzi – with the public streets and piazzas of the city; buildings are portrayed not as isolated objects aloof from the life of the city, but as spatially integrated with public space. Aldo Rossi, one of the prominent participants, reconstituted the Antonine Baths by repairing its structure and adding new buildings to it, making no attempt to connect with Rome's plan.[7] Colin Rowe was one of the few participants to argue for the extension of the complex grain of existing urban blocks to achieve a spatial continuity of streets and squares. As a co-author with Fred Koetter of Collage City (1975)[8] Colin Rowe had already established his theoretical credentials with respect to the collaging of cities, and his designs on Rome – supported by a team of younger designers – suggested how new urban blocks could be shaped to establish a formal continuity with the existing historic spaces.

Roma Interrotta was published as a sequel to the ideas presented by Rodrigo Pérez de Arce in the previous year. In 'Urban Transformations and the Architecture of Additions' Pérez de Arce advocated growth by additive transformation – as opposed to extension or substitution – itself a brilliant extension of Rossi's urban thesis.[9] Pérez de Arce demonstrated how the buildings of antiquity and the spaces of ancient cities had been reused by subsequent inhabitants. The lesson was that old and new buildings can and should co-exist through imaginative adaptation to preserve continuity and, therefore, that modern buildings ought to engage with the pre-existing.

Allies was persuaded by Pérez de Arce's way of thinking. He focused on the huge piazza fronting St Peter's at the Vatican, where Bernini had transformed a structure of

Giulio Romano, Palazzo Te, Mantua

Nolli's Plan of Rome

St Peter's, Rome, before intervention by Bernini

Campidoglio, Rome, before intervention by Michelangelo

Admiral Court Housing, 1992, front and rear elevations

temporary awnings into the permanent stone elliptical colonnades that stand there today. At a smaller scale, but for a space of equal significance for Rome, Allies explored how Michelangelo transformed the haphazardly asymmetrical medieval buildings and public space of the Campidoglio. What impressed him (and Morrison also) was that Michelangelo – famous in equal measure for virtuoso brilliance and temperamental arrogance – had nonetheless ingeniously engaged both the existing medieval buildings on the site and the surviving Roman equestrian statue of Marcus Aurelius, while also articulating, through the convex, elliptical paving in the centre of the space, the ancient significance of the site as omphalos or centre of the Roman state. The result is a work in which the past and the present are conjoined to create a moment of rare urban intensity.

Allies and Morrison's inspired conversion of an unremarkable 1940s concrete and brick warehouse at Butler's Wharf in London's Docklands to create The Clove Building (1990) is an early example of how they could extract what is valuable from the past for the benefit of the present. They gave this former warehouse a character suitable to a mixture of residential, retail, office and public uses, through a partial and selective demolition of its frame, the subtle articulation of its openings, and the addition of new details. This was achieved without concealing what the building once was, yet it is without doubt a better building for the transformation, both visually and in its contribution to its revitalised urban setting. It clearly demonstrates the advantages of growth by additive transformation over extension or substitution.

The same is true of the Admiral Court housing scheme of 1992, which involved the renovation of a late eighteenth-century terrace in Blandford Street, Marylebone. Here they restored the fronts of the terrace and transformed the rear, adding new stair towers and windows of various shapes, which are unified by a white rendered wall. Internally, the blend of old and new is carried through into the interior detailing. The front rooms facing the street are detailed with traditional plaster cornices and panelled joinery, while the rear rooms have flush modern detailing. The contrast of periods is resolved calmly. Old walls retain their regular character and are contrasted with the more freely composed elevations of the new, while the simple palette of white walls and hardwood floors unify the interiors.

Bob Allies and Graham Morrison speak of the search for a resolution in each project they undertake, often defined by a special place in the design. The word they use for this place of resolution is 'stasis' – literally the stoppage of flow, but architecturally the position in a building where one has the sense of arrival – a point of equilibrium where time, motion, the horizontal and vertical are harmoniously resolved. This once had a sacred and universal dimension to it, the omphalos of antiquity being the navel or centre of the world: and there were also lesser, more localised versions of this one 'great centre'. Today, even through the veil of modern scepticism, we can still sense something of the power and presence of particular places. This is certainly something that Allies and Morrison believe, and the cross-hair lines they draw on their site plans indicate its notional position in each design they make.

If the horizontal dimension is Allies's primary interest, the vertical is predominantly Morrison's concern: the grading, texturing and layering of vertical surface. The potential of light, and its corollary shadow, was demonstrated most potently for him in Finland. In contrast to the intense physical layering of the horizontal in Rome, Helsinki sits lightly on a neutral, open but orderly grid. Indeed, the pursuit of lightness is an obvious descriptor for Finnish architecture. The extreme northern light has changing qualities; in contrast to the constant golden light of Italy, it burns bright – brilliant white – into the long summer nights and, as it carries little heat with it, it is welcomed within building interiors. Aalto allowed light to caress and modulate his buildings, designing undulating surfaces that de-laminate from the exterior walls of the building enclosure and creating separate rooms within rooms. While stopping short of Aalto's liking for the sinuous (which rarely suits the tightly regulated site boundaries of urban Britain), Allies and Morrison have adapted many of the devices that he employed to exploit the natural qualities of light for both the surface of their buildings and their interiors.

Their meeting-point as designers is at the rectilinear frame of the building, which they employ as more than a technical structure of support. It has provided them with a representational interface – literally a framework – for their design process, offering discipline and rigour to the plan and scale as well as proportion and meaning to the elevation. The precedents they were drawn to in Rome and Finland demonstrated how such a union was possible. Morrison cites in particular Alvar Aalto's Academic Bookshop in Helsinki (1962-69), while Allies speaks of Franco Albini and Franca Helg's La Rinascente Department Store in Rome (1957-61).

From a distance, Aalto's corner-sited bookstore appears as a simple copper-clad frame glazed by a large, unarticulated single sheet of glass. The treatment of the elevation is at first glance quite stark in its apparent simplicity but its finesse is evident at close quarters. The main, longer elevation is subtly different from that on the side street, its openings being edged, at top and sides, by recessed strips of white travertine marble. On both elevations the copper surfaces are relieved by a tracery of raised copper bands, arranged in pairs like rails, which rise vertically between the windows and horizontally beneath their sills, with louvres to the vertical rails between the windows.

Albini-Helg's La Rinascente building also combines distant simplicity and close-up refinement. Like Aalto's bookstore, its formal outline is rectilinear but the overall impact of the building is quite different. An exposed horizontal steel structure is set proud of an undulating (mainly solid and terracotta-coloured) corrugated curtain wall. Windows are limited to the front-end elevation and they hang as simple glassy sheets from the primary steel frame in front of the curtain wall. La Rinascente also meets the sky differently with a reinterpretation in steel of a palazzo-style renaissance cornice.

To a greater or lesser extent, the architectural language of both buildings derives from the Italian Renaissance. Albini-Helg were building on the edge of Rome, opposite the former Porta Salaria. The site called for a strong wall-like building, of which there are numerous renaissance precedents in Rome, and that city suggested the special character of their design. Helg records that: 'What we set out to do in this dense urban environment was to give the building a status which was not necessarily monumental but was neither dull nor insignificant. It was to have an architectural character and dignity of its own, and at the same time respect the existing norms […]. Things that have been created and made by others, both ancient and modern, are all within our experience, they form part of us, and in our designs emerge as a heritage which belongs to the architectural culture of all of us.'[10]

As a young man Aalto had made a grand tour of Italy, and the buildings of Alberti and Palladio particularly excited him. His Worker's Club at Jyväskylä, Finland (1924) incorporates a Palladian-style window on the first floor facade and also, internally, a giant curved wall decorated with geometrical motifs, inspired by Alberti's sepulchre for the Rucellai chapel at San Pancrazio in Florence.[11] He also knew of a modern exemplar close to home that drew on the classical tradition of European architecture: the extension to the Palladian-style law courts at Gothenburg

Alvar Aalto, Academic Bookshop, Helsinki, 1969

La Rinascente, Rome, Albini-Helg, 1961

(1913-37) by his Swedish contemporary and friend, Gunnar Asplund. This design demonstrates how the essence of western classicism could be edited and simplified to achieve a modern character. Asplund's earliest designs for the additions are Palladian but the final building is quite evidently modern, the extension's block-like form being articulated by an exposed concrete frame with rendered or glass panels placed between. It is a building that both Allies and Morrison admire for its modern assimilation of classical European values.

The authority of the classic modernist designs of Albini and Helg, Aalto and Asplund is most evident in the unbuilt Allies and Morrison project for the Minories office building in London (1990). It has a tripartite – and essentially classical – composition, with horizontal divisions into base, middle and top. A 'piano nobile' is suggested by the detail of the fenestration at first-floor level; the top 'attic' floor is set back from the main fenestration and its canopy acts as a cornice; while the facing grid of the building combines a primary structuring of Portland stone overlaid by a fine grid of metal tramlines, reminiscent of Aalto's bookstore. The elemental quality of Aalto's frame – its tracery of metal tramlines – is captured in the office building at the Nunnery Square business park in Sheffield (1995). Here the frame has the quality of filigree and is set forward of the glass curtain wall that encloses the building proper. Transparency and the articulation of light are twin objectives, with the screen both acting as a brise-soleil to the building's interior and providing a dissolving backdrop to the trees in its park-like setting. This is a building of light and shadow that can dissolve into the landscape while reflecting and emitting different qualities of light by day and night.

By contrast, the Minories was designed to have an urban presence, and unlike the Aalto and Albini prototypes, it was intended to participate in the vitality of the street.

British Embassy, Dublin, 1995

Allies and Morrison place a circular column on the street to mark the glazed entrance doors behind while to the left (vertically to conceal the lift shaft) and right the Portland stone turns from frame to wall. The depth of this wall is emphasised by small, incised windows with sculpted reveals, reminiscent of another major architect whose influence they acknowledge, Carlo Scarpa.

Scarpa's own sources were diverse, ranging from Frank Lloyd Wright, through Japanese art and landscapes to the paintings of Klee and Mondrian,[12] and although his architecture is visually more complex Allies and Morrison are sympathetic to the formal principles on which it is based. For example, Scarpa's Banca Popolare in Verona (1973-78, completed after his death) has a complex tripartite facade whose street level is articulated independently of its middle and top. At street level there is a solid stone wall set forward of the middle storeys and edged by a geometricised string cornice; the main entrance cuts through this wall into the interior. Above, a middle band of marble render floats forward of a glazed screen (which is visible through circular and rectangular windows cut through the render), and has bay windows protruding out of it. The top floor has pairs of metal colonnettes of steel and bronze with mosaic inlays, with setback windows in-between supporting a shallow metal cornice. The rear of Admiral Court and the front elevation of the Minories are less frenetic interpretations of this composition and – again, in the context of Georgian London – are all the more successful for their relative composure.

The vertical stone-covered lift shaft of the Minories acts as a foil to the adjacent building while the setbacks of the sculpted wall at street-level reflect the chaotic vibrancy and scale of human movement. Had it been constructed, the Minories would have achieved urbanistically what Allies and Morrison admire about the Aalto and Albini-Helg prototypes, responding directly to the hierarchy and order of the existing urban structure and sustaining and re-invigorating the urban matrix of which it was part. The building by Carlo Scarpa that perhaps has had the greatest significance for Allies and Morrison is the well-known Castelvecchio Museum at Verona (1956-73). Scarpa's transformation of part of the existing castle into galleries and the location of the equestrian statue on a high pedestal at one end recall Michelangelo's reorganisation of the Campidoglio in Rome. Michelangelo contained the space around the equestrian statue of Marcus Aurelius with buildings, both new and transformed, and provided a new flight of stairs that led directly up to the piazza and the statue at its centre. Scarpa's approach at the Castelvecchio is spatially more complex, exploring the three-dimensionality of Klee and Mondrian. The equestrian statue of Cangrande is elevated – like the Marcus Aurelius – though it cannot be reached directly by a flight of stairs. Instead, the visitor has at first to move away from the statue, to the entrance at the other end of the building, and then through the gallery spaces before arriving at the three-dimensional 'piazza' – of steps, landings and bridges – levelled around it. Using complex horizontal and vertical planes, supports and overhangs, Scarpa frames the Cangrande in space, placing it out of reach. It is situated at a conjunction of opposites, of ancient and new walls, horizontal beams and inclined roof, which the statue as focal point brings into equilibrium.

The poise evident in this juggling and balancing act, as well as the principal components of the overall composition – overlapping walls and planes, feathered roofs and sheet metal emerging from under roof tiles – are referred to in Allies and Morrison's design for the British Embassy in Dublin (1995). Layers of granite block, grey sheet metal and glass similarly connect and overlap, though the wall planes of the embassy are fragmented – their weight negated – by a metal frame developed from the Minories facade. This frame lightens the formality and representational weight of the granite walls, leaving intact the authority necessary to this building type. Like Scarpa, Allies and Morrison use grids and frames not to express directly the structure or construction of the building, but to represent the building's rationale and to ease its relation to the site. To this end, they conceive of the building envelope as a series of discrete layers: the exterior layers express the nature of the building while those of the interior respond to the logic of the plan and section. Their architecture develops from the mismatch and contradictions between outside and in and the rational rhythm of the frame that disciplines both worlds. By striving for a resolution of unequal parts – acknowledging an 'obligation toward the difficult whole' – the Dublin embassy appears neither overblown nor pompous yet it retains the dignity appropriate to its purpose. More relaxed are the areas accessible to the public and general staff, which has a different order of architecture – brick walls layered with granite, metal canopies and grilles – linked by undulating pathways that direct visitors through the landscaped garden.

In essence, the Dublin embassy is a large house. Its domestic core of rooms is a scaled-up version of those in Graham Morrison's own house in Blackheath (1992), formalised to meet the public and institutional status of an embassy. Both 'houses' are dominated by a simple rectangular or linear building block protected by a triangular pitched roof, the ends terminated by square blocks containing a balcony at upper level.

At the embassy, smaller ancillary buildings cluster around this primary form. The ensemble is reminiscent of the grand villas of Palladio's era, the administrative centres of large farming estates, which were used for work and entertainment. Palladio arranged this ensemble according to the belief of contemporary theorists that architecture should respond to the beauty found in nature, particularly the human body. The main 'body' of the building

Castelvecchio Museum, Carlo Scarpa, 1973

Banca Popolare Verona, Carlo Scarpa, 1973

Morrison House, Blackheath, 1992

Abbey Mills Pumping Station, 1997

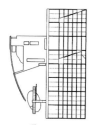
Museum of Contemporary Art, Helsinki, 1993

Sarum Hall School, London, 1995

contained the most important functions, around which the secondary buildings were arranged symmetrically, as if they were its limbs.[13] Such complete symmetry is too formal a device within the modern idiom. But the vernacular farmstead of Finland, the niemelantorppa, has discrete building blocks of varying scale, achieving an informal hierarchy that Allies and Morrison consider appropriate. This relaxed hierarchy of forms was interpreted by Aalto for his own country retreat at Muuratsalo (1953), which has rooms arranged as small buildings that connect with one another organically, achieving a naturalism within the landscape that appears more casual than Palladio's but is no less deliberate.

Again, Allies and Morrison combined what is pertinent from both approaches. They arranged the component parts of the embassy to suggest informality, so that it can be accommodated simply into the rectilinear street patterns of suburban Dublin (a pattern also common to much of northern Europe).

Consequently, asymmetric orthogonals dominate their plans, with the primary block having secondary buildings attached at right angles to it. This T-shaped plan can be found in a number of designs, including the 1993 competition scheme for the National Museum of Contemporary Art, Helsinki, Sarum Hall school in north London (1995) and the small interior of Stephen Bull's Bistro (1992, since demolished). Stripped of its secondary accretions, the linear house form is left exposed in the student residences at Newnham College, Cambridge (1995). In each instance, the idea of house has been re-evaluated: house as museum, as school, as student residence; even dining in the restaurant interior is presented as a domestic experience.

The house analogy also provides the primary language for their Abbey Mills Pumping Station (1997), which is outwardly one of their most original designs.

The geometry of the house-type is inscribed on its gable ends, while chimneys punctuate the roof. But it has then undergone a radical transformation – one that demonstrates the great potential of their approach as a setting for innovation. The familiar model has been dipped in metal and in the process transformed (as ancient wooden temples were transformed by stone and marble). With Abbey Mills, Allies and Morrison produced a design that recognisably extends their thinking. Moreover, it demonstrates that their architecture can meet situation and need by transforming – even transcending – a typology fundamental to the European architectural tradition.

The house motif also draws on the long-established idea that a house is a microcosm of the spaces and activities of a well-ordered city. The so-called 'city-house analogy' is described by Alberti and Palladio as ancient wisdom,[14] and was referred to positively, in very different circumstances, by Alison and Peter Smithson during the life of Team X. It reinforced the belief that cities are for people and should be lived in as the extension of the regulated home. Furthermore, Alberti asked: 'cannot the various parts of the house – atria, xysti (colonnaded open spaces), dining rooms, porticoes, and so on – be considered miniature buildings?'[15] This direct equation suggests, in the modern world, a context for the combination of buildings and spaces that make a city. As the eighteenth-century Nolli plan of Rome revealed, in the most beautiful and inhabitable cities there is a direct relation between the internal spaces of buildings and the connected external public space of the city. Through the city-house analogy, public spaces are to be understood as enlarged living spaces and this is how Allies and Morrison configure them.

In a series of projects – including the British Museum forecourt (1990), the South Bank Centre (1994), Regent Street (1995) and the completed spaces at Liverpool Pierhead (1995) and the garden courts flanking the entrance to Tate Britain (2001) – the public realm is described through devices familiar to the traditional European city. Rectilinear strips and grids of smooth stone and carefully detailed kerbs and contained landscape consistently delineate their spaces. The plans are as carefully contrived as those of buildings to create 'rooms' and geometry provides their arrangement with unity and clarity. The resulting places offer scale, direction and implied containment for human activity and for people moving through them, whether alone or in small and large groups. Again, informality is suggested by asymmetries in plan, while interaction and touch are encouraged by the paraphernalia of urban domesticity – lights, bench seats, bins and planting. To create urban spaces as places Allies and Morrison reinforce the relation between buildings and street at ground level, re-establishing the normal conventions and conditions of urban life.

Of course, the art in all this is not just a matter of observation but also of response and judgement. The experience of great cities and buildings is nothing if architects lack the ability to translate well reasoned ideas into buildings and places of quality. Each situation is unique and interventions need to balance complex demands. There are no ready formulas to apply, and it is the architecture and urban design skills that Allies and Morrison bring to each specific urban situation that distinguishes their approach. Through reasoned speculation they have demonstrated the sensibilities to innovate and the capacity to develop an architecture that many people can participate in. In the end, it is their kind of sensitivity and subtlety that makes European cities pleasurable places to inhabit: grand architectural statements – no matter the virtuosity of their creators – cannot exist without the context that architects like them have laid down for centuries. Theirs is an architecture that, as Aldo Rossi demanded, is conceived as integral to the city, and that acknowledges above all the construction of the city over time.[16]

---

1 As they make clear in Allies, B and G Morrison, 'A Particular Point of View', Michigan Architecture Papers. Map Two: Allies and Morrison, The University of Michigan, Ann Arbor, 1996: 17 (hereafter cited as Allies and Morrison 1996).

2 An aesthetic first popularised by Alison and Peter Smithson: Ordinariness and Light: Urban Theories '52-'60 and their application in a building project '63-'70, Faber & Faber, London 1970; Without Rhetoric: an Architectural Aesthetic 1955-1972, The MIT Press 1973.

3 As in the work of the London-based practice, Caruso St John, whose acclaimed Walsall Gallery completed in 2000 is much closer to the kind of architecture that the Smithsons were promoting.

4 Rossi, A L'architettura della città. The first English edition, The Architecture of the City, (trans D Ghirardo and J Ockman, with an introduction by Peter Eisenman), was published by The MIT Press, 1982. Venturi, R Complexity and Contradiction in Architecture, (with an introduction by Vincent Scully), The Museum of Modern Art Papers on Architecture, 1966.

5 His findings regarding Palazzo Te (better known as Palazzo del Té until the 1980s) were published in the the Architectural Review on his return: Allies, B 'Order, orthodoxy and the orders', Architectural Review, vol 173, no 1036, June 1983, pp59-65.

6 Graves M (ed), AD Profiles 20: Roma Interrotta, Architectural Design, vol 49, no 3-4, 1979.

7 Roma Interrotta, Architectural Design, vol 49, no 3-4, 1979.

8 This first appeared in essay form in Rowe, C and F Koetter, 'Collage City', Architectural Review, CLVIII, 942, August 1975, pp66-91, and was subsequently extended and published by The MIT Press in 1979.

9 Pérez de Arce, R 'Urban Transformations and the Architecture of Additions, AD Profile 12: Urban Transformations, Architectural Design, vol 48, no 4, 1978, pp237-266.

10 After Fiori, L and M Prizzon (eds), Albini-Helg, La Rinascente, Milan 1982, as translated into English in P von Meiss, 'The aesthetics of gravity', arq, vol 4, no 3, 2000, pp243-5.

11 F Dal Co, 'Aalto e Alberti', Casabella, vol 62, no 659, Sept 1998, pp66-75; and R Tavernor, On Alberti and the Art of Building, Yale University Press, 1998, pp106-119.

12 See for example: Manfredo Tafuri, 'Carlo Scarpa and Italian architecture', Carlo Scarpa: The Complete Works, F Dal Co and G Mazzariol (eds), Electa/Architectural Press, 1986, pp72-95, esp p89.

13 R Tavernor, 'Palladio's corpus: I quattro libri dell'architettura', Paper Palaces, V Hart and P Hicks (eds), 1998, pp233-46.

14 See LB Alberti: On the Art of Building in Ten Books, J Rykwert, N Leach and R Tavernor (trans and eds), MIT Press, 1988, p23; Andrea Palladio: The Four Books on Architecture, R Tavernor and R Schofield, (trans and eds), MIT Press, 1997, p122.

15 LB Alberti: On the Art of Building in Ten Books, J Rykwert, N. Leach and R Tavernor (trans and eds), MIT Press, 1988, p23.

16 Rossi, A, The Architecture of the City, (trans D Ghirardo and J Ockman, with an introduction by Peter Eisenman), MIT Press, 1982, p21.

Robert Tavernor is Professor of Architecture and Urban Design and Director of the Cities Programme at the London School of Economics and Political Science (LSE). He is the author of Palladio and Palladianism (1991, Thames & Hudson), On Alberti and the Art of Building (1998, Yale UP), and Smoot's Ear: The Measure of Humanity (2007, Yale UP). He is co-editor of Body and Building: Essays on the Changing Relation of Body and Architecture (2002, MIT Press), and the co-translator and editor of the classic treatises on architecture by Vitruvius, Alberti and Palladio: Leon Battista Alberti: On the Art of Building, in Ten Books (1988, MIT Press), Andrea Palladio: The Four Books on Architecture (1997, MIT Press), and Vitruvius: The Ten Books on Architecture (2009, Penguin Classics).

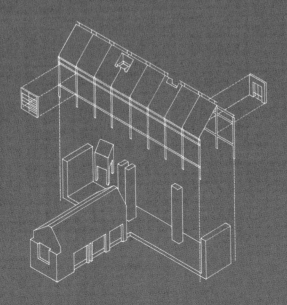

Projects 1983–2003

THE MOUND

Edinburgh
1983–90

The design of the new public landscape at The Mound was the subject of an open architectural competition held in 1983. Bob Allies and Graham Morrison collaborated on a submission, and their selection as winners led to the formation of the practice in 1984.

The Mound had been created in the second half of the eighteenth century as a by-product of the construction of Edinburgh New Town. Excavated material was placed across the valley of the Nor' Loch to form a new connection back to the Old Town. The two public buildings that dominate the site – the National Gallery of Scotland and the Royal Scottish Academy – were constructed on The Mound in the early years of the nineteenth century.

The space around the two buildings had been usurped by cars and parking until, in the 1970s, pedestrianisation was introduced, albeit in a provisional and half-hearted manner. The competition was intended to provide a more permanent and appropriate solution to the site's growing significance as a public space. In contrast to the majority of the other competition

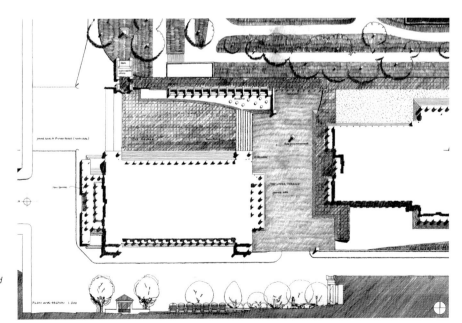

The competition submission comprised two contrasting freehand pencil drawings by Graham Morrison (left) and Bob Allies (right).

The pavilion and kiosks define the edge of a new square.

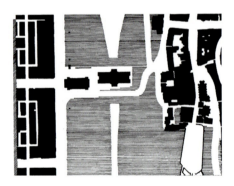

The site forms a link between the contrasting grain of the New Town on the left and the Old Town on the right.

entries, Allies and Morrison focused on the inherent characteristics of the site – the topography of the landscape, the setting of the two galleries (both designed by William Playfair), the routes that draw people into and across the site, and the relationship between The Mound and the adjacent Princes Street Gardens.

The boundary of the gardens was adjusted as part of the proposals and the connection between the gardens and the new square emphasised by the construction of a pavilion that also marked the beginning of the route that connects Princes Street to the Old Town. The design of the pavilion was at once a response to the neoclassicism of the two galleries and a consciously archaic form. Sandstone piers supported a roof of steel trusses with oak eaves and a steel ridge pole. Flush Caithness stone laid with open joints formed the surface of the roof.

Such was the sensitivity of the site that the project was not completed until seven years after the competition. The pavilion was dismantled when the Playfair Project was implemented to refurbish and extend the galleries.

The pavilion and kiosk beyond mark the route from Princes Street to Edinburgh's Old Town.

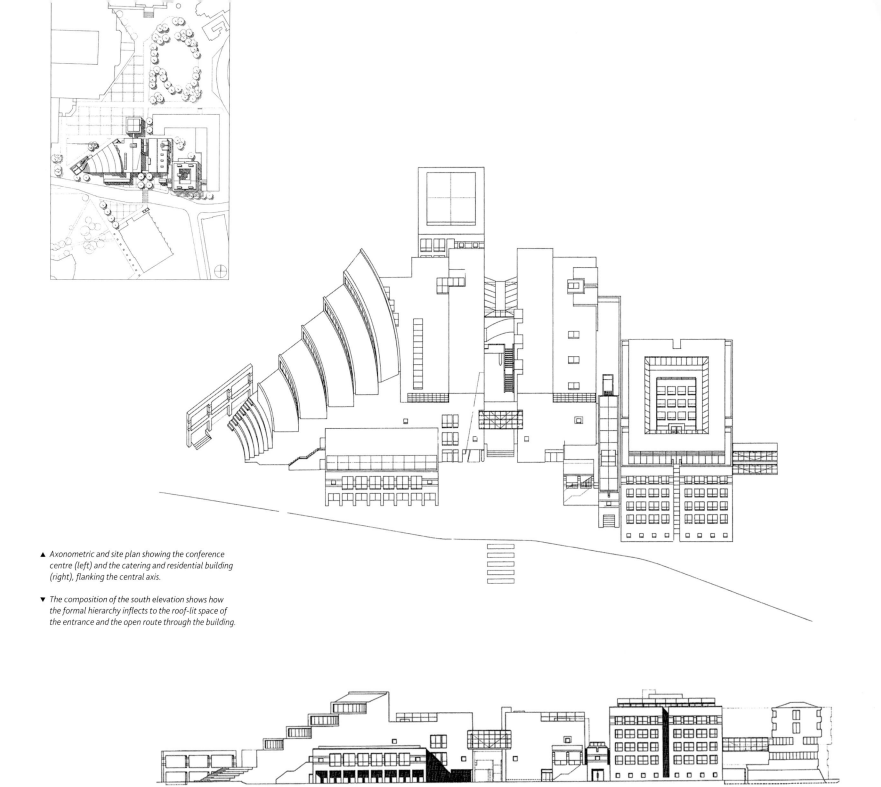

▲ Axonometric and site plan showing the conference centre (left) and the catering and residential building (right), flanking the central axis.

▼ The composition of the south elevation shows how the formal hierarchy inflects to the roof-lit space of the entrance and the open route through the building.

ASTON TRIANGLE

Birmingham
1986

Located at the heart of Aston University, this competition entry for a new University Centre sought to unite the disparate parts of the new campus. The fragmented plan, broken into its constituent parts, provided the possibility of a more complex composition to link the university's existing buildings, to emphasise routes and vistas, and to provide an emblematic assembly of buildings to promote its identity.

A partially glazed mall provides a sheltered entrance to the conference centre and establishes a formal link between the existing student union and the library. While the symmetrical residential building completes a courtyard with the management centre, the roof of the new auditorium steps down to form an external amphitheatre facing the main university entrance. Seminar rooms and support areas are accommodated in separate but linked pavilions.

Much of the ground floor frontage of the individual buildings is given over to shops and cafes to enliven the principal routes. A generous stair and glass lift lead from the entrance to the principal floor where all of the new facilities are integrated. Although the dominant external material is red brick like the neighbouring university buildings, the mall, main staircase enclosure and first-floor bridge are detailed in white-painted metal and render in recognition of their internal roles. The separate seminar pavilion is also finished in white to add significance to the new university square.

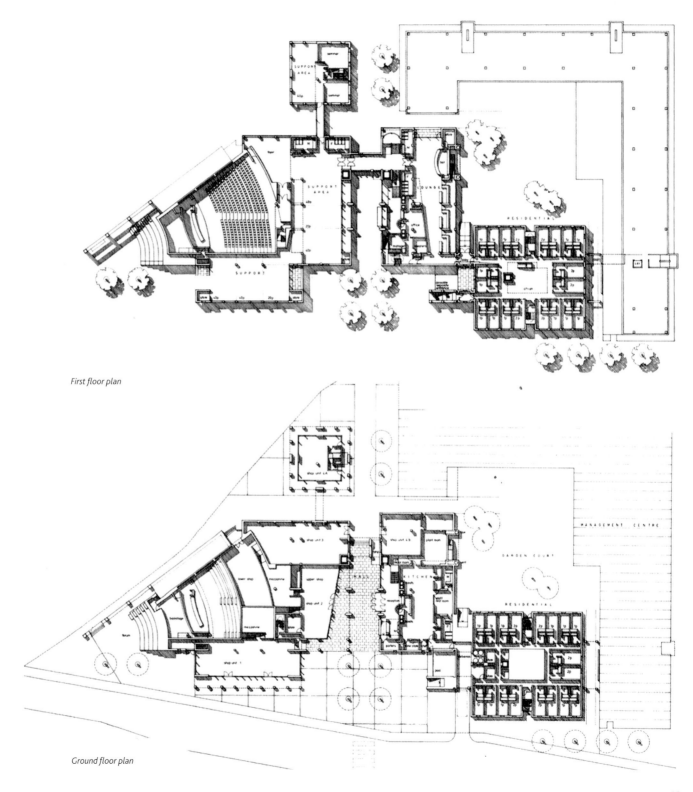

First floor plan

Ground floor plan

THE CLOVE BUILDING
Butler's Wharf, London
1987–90

Constructed only as far as its first-floor level in the late 1930s, Building 10 (now the Clove Building) was used as a gun emplacement during the wartime defence of London's docks, prior to its hurried completion when safe trade recommenced in 1945. The original five-floor warehouse was designed to carry heavy loads, with a structural grid of mushroom-head columns supporting a continuous flat slab. It extends the full depth of the plot between Maguire Street and the winding Shad Thames in the newly designated Butler's Wharf district.

◀ *The tripartite order of the adjusted Maguire Street facade showing the retained structure (left) and the new addition (right) that steps back to signal the entrance.*
▼ *Site plan and concept diagram.*

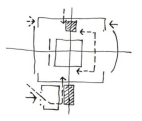

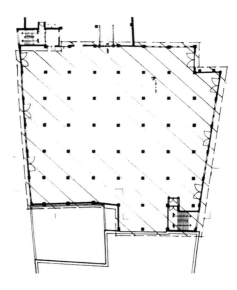
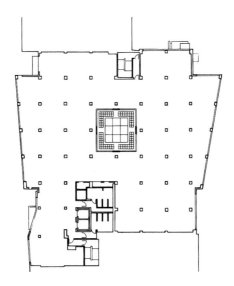
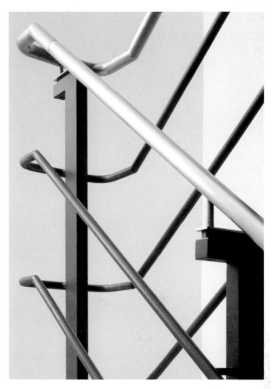

Floor plans of the existing building on the left and the adjusted building on the right.

The redeveloped building contains shops with street entrances, car parking and a reception space. From the entrance a stair links directly to a new first-floor gallery (envisaged as a potential link to the adjacent Design Museum) and four levels of studio office space that surround a new central courtyard.

The selective demolition of the building's corners reveals the presence of an inner orthogonal geometry that appears separate from the remaining splayed walls on the building line. This is emphasised by the addition of a new top floor that extends this plane. The removal of the central four structural bays down to the first floor has allowed the creation of a courtyard that brings natural light to the studio floors and to the 'roof' of the first-floor gallery. In addition the fortuitous addition to the project of a small adjacent site has enabled an entrance and core building to be added that remains distinct from the original warehouse structure.

The building has three facades. The west elevation, with the new attached entrance articulated against the remaining four-bay facade of the warehouse, faces Maguire Street. Here the shop fronts are in the plane

Elevation to Shad Thames Square with projecting balconies overlooking the street.

of the facade. The warehouse facade is replicated on the much narrower Shad Thames to the east, but here the ground floor forms a colonnade and the pavement is brought within the facade, following a new curved metal and glass shop front and leading to the new Shad Thames Square to the north east. Here a small part of the building is exposed to form a third facade, the proportions of which appear almost domestic. The upper floors open onto small metal balconies that overlook the new square.

The tripartite composition of the white-rendered facades reflects the building's new uses. The shops and gallery occupy the base, the three existing floors intended for studio use form the middle, and the new attic level provides a studio floor, with wide spans on slender columns opening onto terraces enclosed by the extended frame of the building facade. The lower, subordinate facade of the new core building is inflected to reveal the inner orthogonal layer and a metal canopy marks the entrance.

Constructional detail is kept simple and external materials are restricted to white-painted render and metal windows and balustrades painted a uniform warm metallic grey; oak is used sparingly to cap the balustrades.

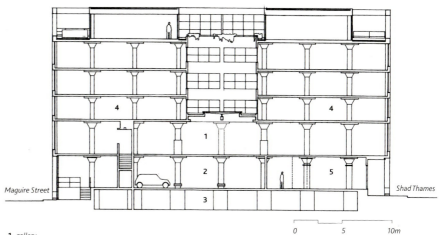

1 gallery
2 parking
3 storage
4 offices
5 shop

▲ A three-storey light well was introduced to facilitate cross ventilation to the office spaces and provide daylight to the first-floor gallery. A new top floor was added behind the extended frame of the original structure.
▶ A framed roof terrace caps the entrance at the junction between the old and new structure.

FELSTED SCHOOL
Essex
1987

The proposed dining hall and staff facilities for Felsted School, near Great Dunmow in Essex, are housed in a new building linked to the existing school buildings by a series of outdoor spaces arranged on either side of a public road. Further enclosure is provided by a new cloister walk, similar to that in the main school, forming an extended covered entrance to the dining hall.

Externally, the building is intended to suggest the form and scale of a traditional dining hall, with a steel frame structure clad in slate and red brick with stone dressings.

Internally, however, by placing the staff accommodation within the substantial roof space, with the major rooms occupying the gable ends, the character has been rendered more domestic than institutional, in accordance with the client's brief.

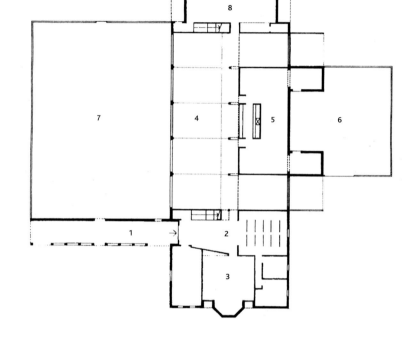

Ground floor plan

1 *cloister*
2 *entrance*
3 *common room*
4 *dining room*
5 *kitchen*
6 *deliveries*
7 *garden*
8 *staff dining*

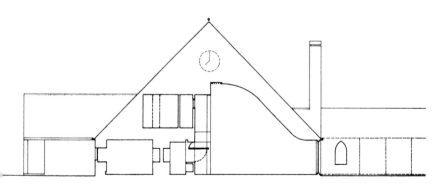

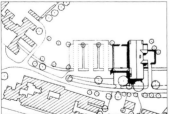

The cloister, which marks the entrance to the dining hall and provides shelter for queuing, also defines the edge of a garden.

SAINSBURY'S SUPERMARKET
Competition
1987

This proposal was made for an international open ideas competition sponsored by Sainsbury and the Architectural Review for the design of an out-of-town supermarket.

The proposition was that, although intended for a rural or semi-rural site, the supermarket as a building type might nevertheless borrow from the city a sense of order, and establish a normally lacking legibility with an organisation that is easy to understand and therefore easy to use.

The primary strategy was the introduction of an intermediate external cloister separating the car park from the building and forming a threshold appropriate in scale to the spaces and uses on either side. As a place of safety for children, and of tranquility, the cloister would form part of a clear assembly of elements, including a car park, the supermarket and a petrol station, that would be visible from the adjacent elevated motorway, and comprehensible on the ground.

Dominating the composition of the supermarket was the roof, a simple sloping enclosure articulated only by sections of roof glazing that allow light through an elliptical diffuser into the sales area below. The interior space was shaped and oriented by a light, reflective awning suspended from steel trusses supported by two central columns.

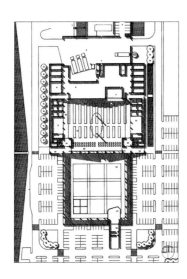

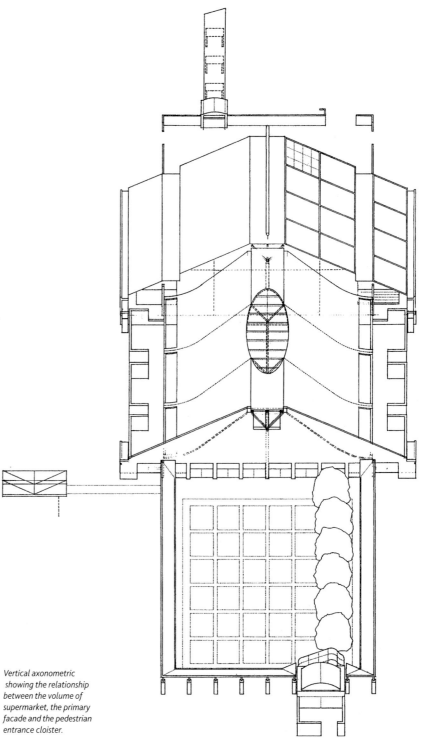

Vertical axonometric showing the relationship between the volume of supermarket, the primary facade and the pedestrian entrance cloister.

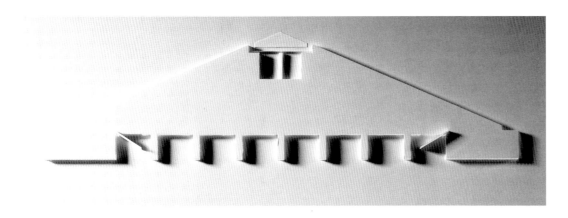

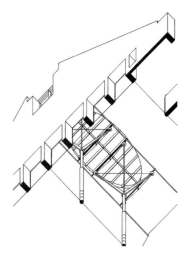

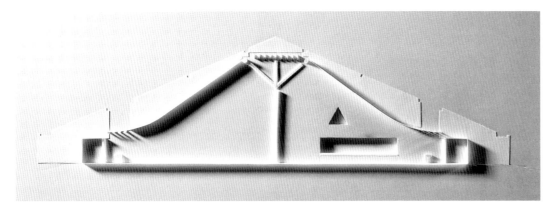

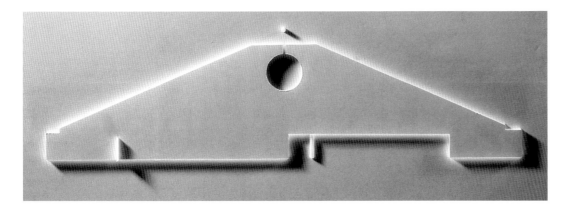

▲ Upview axonometric showing the canopied interior and central oval rooflight.
◀ Card relief models of the entrance facade, cross section and rear facade. The entrance facade acknowledges the order of the cloister whereas the rear facade appears pragmatic and informal.

   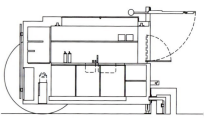

Existing ice cream kiosk at the British Museum.   *Detail from Piranesi drawing of a hay cart (1757).*   *Tea trolley designed by Alvar Aalto (1936-37).*   *Cross section of the proposed kiosk.*

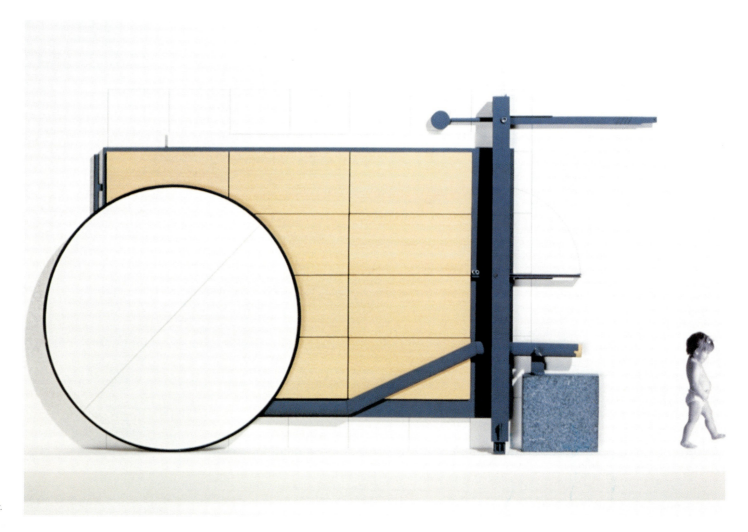

Relief model of the proposed ice cream kiosk.

BRITISH MUSEUM FORECOURT
London
1990

This hypothetical proposal for the design of a new ice cream kiosk at the British Museum was undertaken as part of the Rediscovering the Public Realm exhibition, curated by Deyan Sudjic, at the RIBA's Heinz Gallery. An existing glass-fibre kiosk then dominated visitors' first impressions of the museum as they passed through the imposing cast-iron screen that separates the courtyard from the street.

The focus of the scheme was provided by a large paved square in the centre of the forecourt, replacing the narrow axial tarmac path that previously connected the entrance gates to the main portico. To open up the space to more extensive public use, additional entrances were proposed to the west and east with the primary visitor approach from the west being acknowledged by a new asymmetry in the plan.

Within this new landscape – from which car parking was eliminated – positions were identified for the necessary seats and litter bins, and the new ice cream kiosk was allocated a specific location.

The kiosk was conceived as a temporary structure capable of being wheeled away at the end of the summer season. Its giant wheel was intended to make the temporary nature explicit while its formal composition grew out of the detail of its various components – counter, canopy and shutter.

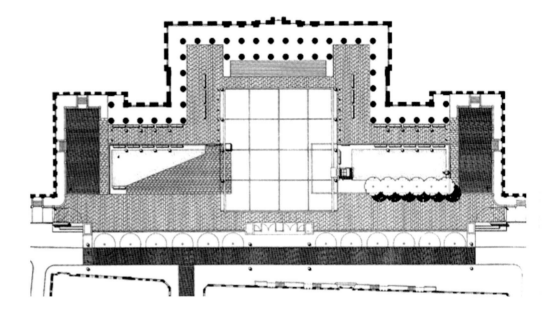

Plan of the proposed entrance forecourt

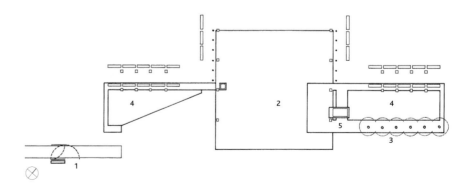

Diagram showing components of the new landscape

1 *new entrance gates*
2 *York stone paving*
3 *granite setts*
4 *lawn*
5 *ice cream kiosk*

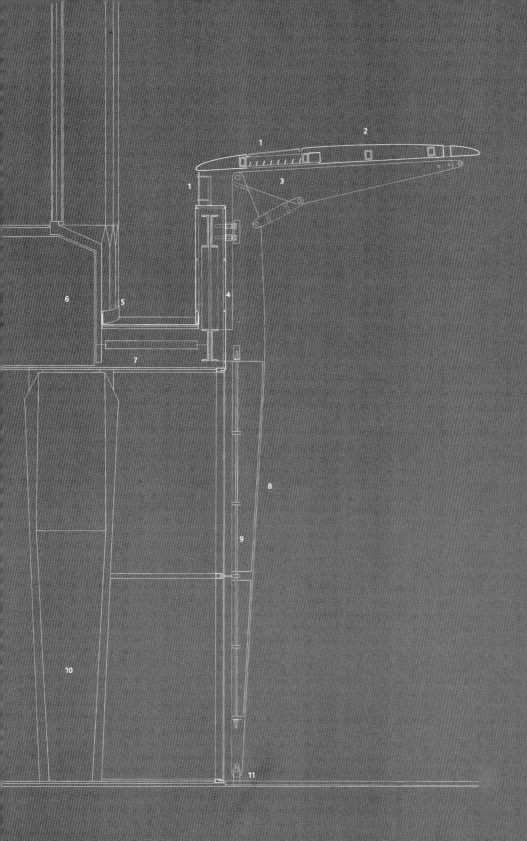
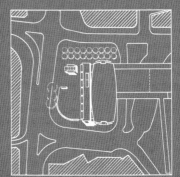

1 planar glazing
2 metal-clad windshelf
3 louvres
4 metal cladding
5 waterproof wind channel
6 existing concrete slab
7 structural tie to existing building
8 painted metal L-frame
9 double glazing panels
10 existing X-column
11 sliding connection to ground-floor slab

CENTRE POINT WINDSHELF
London
1988–90

While Richard Seifert's 1964 office tower is a familiar landmark on London's skyline, Centre Point's relationship to its immediate context has always been problematic. The 35-storey building sits on a windswept island cut off from its surroundings by a sea of traffic.

This proposal created an accessible public square in front of the building as well as a simplified pattern of traffic circulation around the podium. This change involved the removal of the existing car park ramp in order to make way for a ground-level entrance hall and allowed full access to the building for disabled visitors. To protect users of the building from wind turbulence at the base of the tower, the new enclosure to the entrance hall incorporated a windshelf across the full width of the facade. Because of constraints at basement level, the steel structure was to be supported by a concrete beam at first-floor level, with pin joints locating the bases of the steel cantilevers at ground level. The delicate steel structure was shaped by structural performance requirements while its propped cantilever extended the primary beam to the ground.

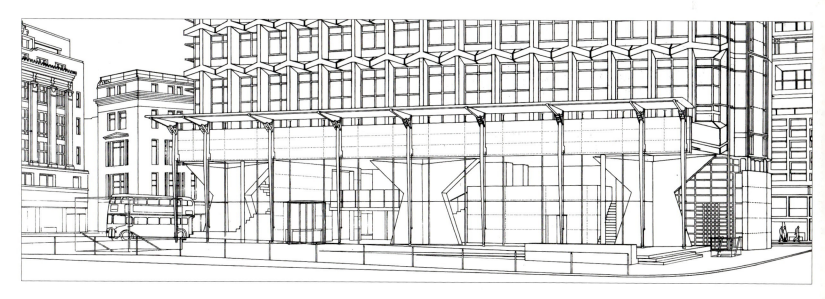

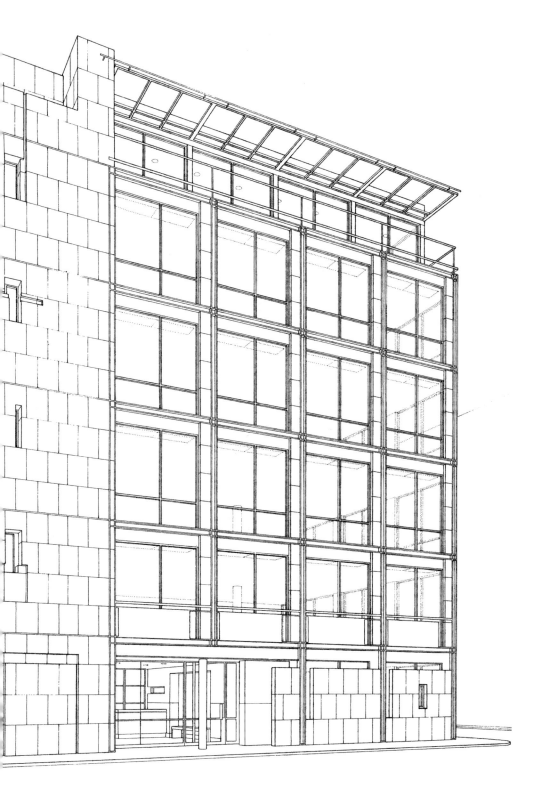

MINORIES
London
1990

This project was an attempt to resolve and exploit the tensions between the needs of a commercial office building with a repetitive 1.5-metre planning grid, and the essential urban character of its setting in the City of London.

The six-storey form is determined both by the restrictions in plan of the small corner site and by the height of the adjacent buildings. The core, placed against the party wall, helps maximise the efficiency of the plan and allows the entrance to face the Minories, the major street.

A modelled metal frame, reflecting the three-metre structural grid, generates the composition of both elevations and dominates the corner. The addition of Portland stone to the Minories facade and a metal layer to the India Street facade reflect the relative importance of each street, reasserting the existing urban hierarchy. Where the new building abuts its neighbours, intermediate bays of stone or brick are placed in the continuous but simplified elevational frame to give opacity where needed and to ease the transition. The minimal fenestration in these panels, though seemingly random, acknowledges the facades of the adjacent buildings.

Like its neighbours, the building adopts a tripartite division of base, middle and pavilion top. The comparative complexity of the ground-level composition is countered on the first floor by a more solid balustrade, while the top floor is set back to allow a fully glazed facade with terraces that overlook the Minories. Mechanical plant is grouped at roof level in the centre of the plan, and the resulting informal composition of structural and service elements above the cornice provides a rich and complex profile.

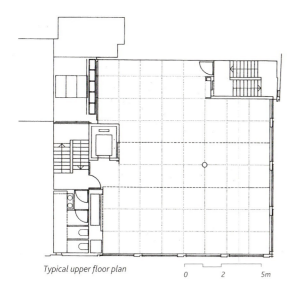

Typical upper floor plan

0 2 5m

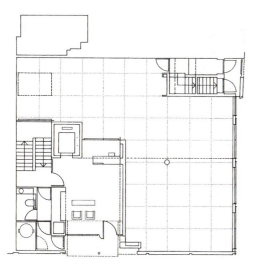

Ground floor plan

The masonry enclosure of the new core mediates between the fenestration of the adjacent building and the repetitive bays of the new structure.

DULWICH PICTURE GALLERY
London
1990

Dulwich Picture Gallery, the first public art gallery in England, was designed by John Soane in 1811 and opened in 1817. Over the years a series of additions and extensions were made, including a major renovation following wartime damage by a flying bomb. But public facilities remained sparse until, in 1990, an architectural competition was held to explore how the building might be extended to better accommodate visitors.

The original building is set in an enclosed garden surrounded by a row of Georgian houses to the east, open fields to the west and almshouses to the north. Symmetrical and self-contained, it did not invite accretions.

Rather than compromise Soane's gallery by building alongside it, Allies and Morrison proposed the construction of a separate pavilion located along the College Road frontage, immediately adjacent to the entrance. This established a new enclosing wall to the site and reinforced the sense of an entrance courtyard already implied by the almshouses and, indeed, anticipated in some of Soane's early sketches for the museum. For the visitor arriving at the gallery, Soane's building would continue to dominate the approach while on departure the entrance to the new pavilion would in turn be immediately apparent. Beyond, the glazed wall of the cafe would open out towards the gardens.

Within the new building the functions of reception, bookshop, tea room and multipurpose hall were arranged to reduce unnecessary circulation, encourage flexibility in use and minimise the level of security supervision. A separate entrance provided access directly from College Road to the education

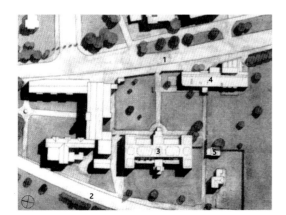

1 *College Road*
2 *Gallery Road*
3 *Dulwich Picture Gallery*
4 *proposed pavilion*
5 *proposed framing workshop*

John Soane's original Picture Gallery continues to dominate the composition in Allies and Morrison's proposal, but the new building to the south-east (top right) adds definition to the enclosure of the gardens.

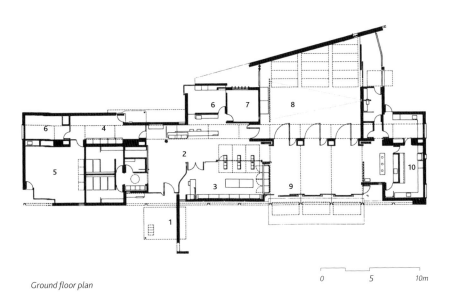

Ground floor plan

0 5 10m

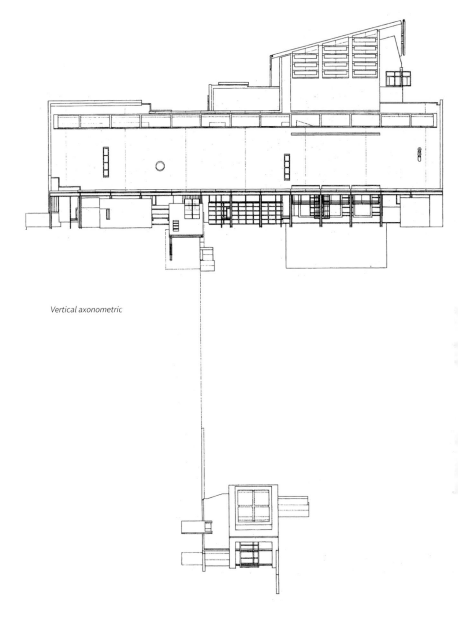

Vertical axonometric

1 entrance
2 reception
3 shop
4 school entrance
5 education room
6 office
7 staff room
8 multipurpose hall
9 tea room
10 kitchen

rooms, allowing the pavilion to be used discretely for private functions when the Picture Gallery was closed to the public. A smaller pavilion containing a new picture framing workshop was positioned adjacent to the main gallery, with independent servicing from Gallery Road. The enclosing walls of the new building were to be London stock brick with a combination of oak and steel windows. The garden elevation was framed in steel with large glazed openings to the education room, reception and tea room protected by a brise-soleil and security grilles.

The perspective drawing illustrates the layered transitional space at the entrance.

SCOTT HOWARD BUILDING
Kings Cross, London
1988–91

This showroom and offices for a furniture company was built on the site of a previously demolished eighteenth-century church designed by Aaron Hurst. Because of the significance of the setting, a planning agreement established when the original building was demolished required that any new building on the site should replicate the form of the original structure.

St James' Church had comprised a simple brick enclosure with a slate roof and white-painted stucco details to the main frontage. The new building follows this configuration, with the main facade designed as a close replica, while the side elevations respond to the specific interior requirements of the new use.

Within the brick envelope the white interior – floors and cores – are set back from the perimeter walls to create two double-height spaces, one of which forms the entrance hall. The white interior is acknowledged within the facade by a layer of grey metal which incorporates the window frames, and this intermediate layer is revealed within the depth of the masonry openings.

The simple rectangular plan arrangement incorporates open 15-metre by 18-metre floorplates with stair and service cores at each end. However, the sectional design creates a variety of spaces on each of the floors with changing relationships to the volume contained behind the main facade.

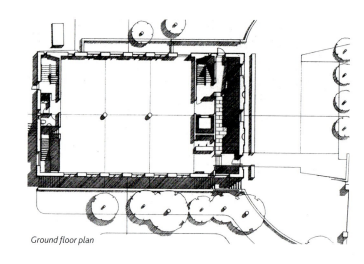

Ground floor plan

◀ *Detail from John O'Connor's 1884 painting of Pentonville Road with St James' Church in the foreground (Museum of London).*
◀ *The reconstructed brick and stucco facade.*
▶ *The double-height entrance hall links the ground floor and basement level.*

LIBRARY, UNIVERSITY OF ESSEX
Colchester
1991

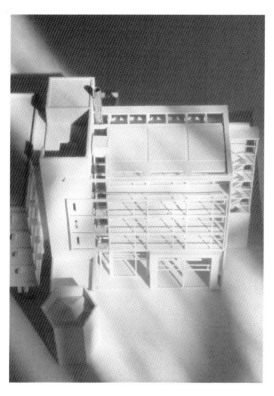

Model of new building as extension to existing concrete-framed library.

The existing library at the University of Essex is housed in a six-storey concrete and glass structure characteristic of the 1960s campus. The proposed extension, to the west of the existing building, employs a similar architectural vocabulary but with subtle modifications.

The rectangular building consists of six floors of book stacks and study areas, plus a circulation tower that articulates these spaces with the existing library. The full-height roof-lit space gathers the main horizontal and vertical circulation routes and the staff desk is relocated to this new centre of gravity.

At ground level the extension comprises a double-height space housing catalogues, microfilm readers and the reference collection. Library offices and a conference room are positioned under a mezzanine that incorporates study areas overlooking the main space. As in the existing library, the floors of stacks above consist of large, uninterrupted spaces in which flexibility and efficiency are maximised by locating subsidiary elements – lifts, escape stairs, toilets and service risers – at the perimeter.

The extension differs significantly from the original library in the nature and arrangement of reader spaces. A clear distinction is made between the open-plan arrangement of tables and chairs, with views north-east towards the campus lakes, and the enclosed individual carrels to the south-west. The substance and simplicity of the original library suggested a model for the new interior. The structure of the new building is of reinforced concrete with in-situ columns and beams and precast floor slabs. On the south-west elevation, a lattice of concrete piers provides enclosure and shading to the individual study carrels. As in

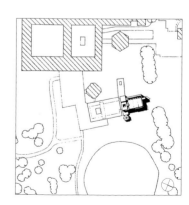

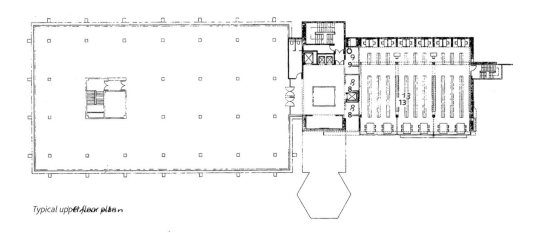

Typical upper floor plan

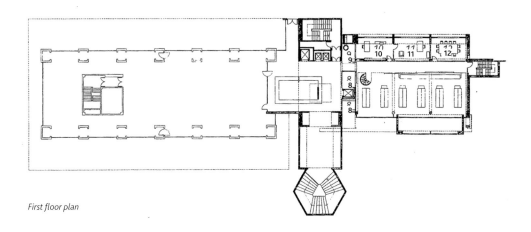

First floor plan

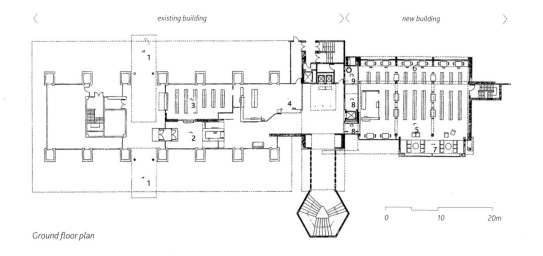

Ground floor plan

1 *entrance canopy*
2 *security desk*
3 *short-loan collection*
4 *circulations desk*
5 *reference*
6 *reading tables*
7 *informal seating*
8 *void*
9 *service riser*
10 *librarian*
11 *secretary*
12 *seminar room*
13 *book stacks*

the existing library, the interior of the extension comprises fair-faced concrete, glass, and wood panelling in both the offices and the carrels.

Current standards of insulation and environmental performance made it inappropriate to replicate the construction of the original building. The extension is therefore faced with an insulated metal cladding system with integrated double glazing and opening lights. The external envelope inflects toward the original building and is designed to minimise, or potentially eliminate, the need for mechanical ventilation or air conditioning to the library floors. While glazing is extensive on the north-east elevation, it is mostly limited to high levels on the south-west side so as to reduce solar gain and to maximise reflected natural light and cross-ventilation. Small desk-level windows allow for additional individually controlled ventilation as well as giving views out to the campus.

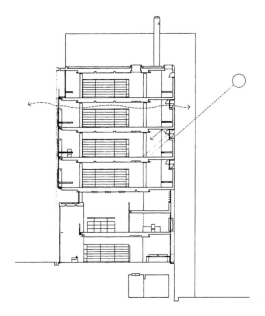

Cross section

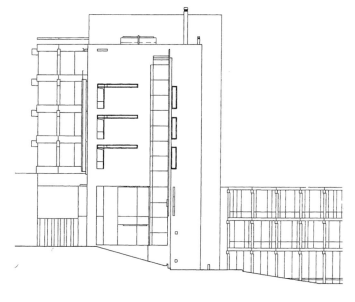

North-west elevation

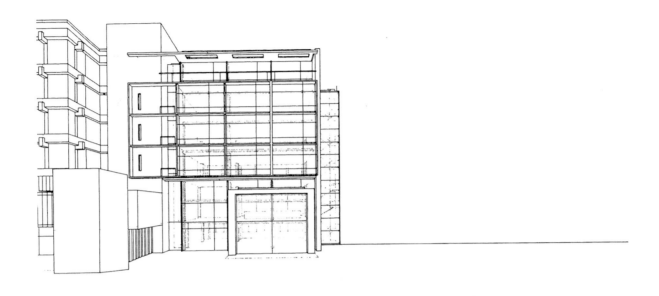

North-east perspective

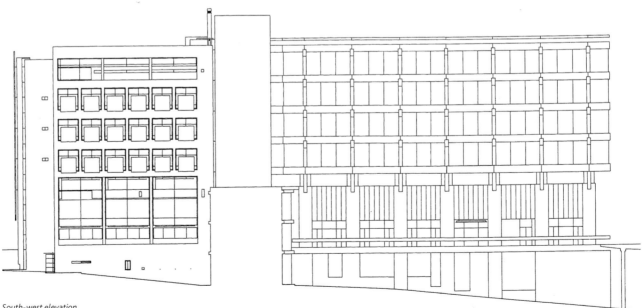

South-west elevation

OAK YARD
Blackheath, London
1992

The design of an architect's own house can provide the opportunity to demonstrate an architectural position, to develop compositional thinking and to consider the role and significance of the detailed design. At Oak Yard in Blackheath, Graham Morrison explores the relationship between the traditional and the modern, as well a compositional asymmetry and the layering and hierarchy of constructional detail.

Three primary elements – the floating slate roof, a solid brick enclosure and a projecting white-painted porch – refer to the context of late-Georgian and early-Victorian pedimented villas in Blackheath. Built on a sloping, irregularly shaped site among a group of mature trees, the house has a 6.6-metre deep plan and is organised about a symmetrical structural spine that rises through its three storeys.

The porch, a formal counterpart to the white-plastered interior, extends forward to provide a brick-paved outdoor 'room' a few steps above street level. A similar paved court in the garden comprises a larger terrace into which a room-sized space is inscribed. The terraces establish a plinth for the simple brick facades that envelop the white interior

The house looks over existing communal gardens.

North, east, south and west elevations

spaces. The volume of the house is articulated at the east gable to form a shallow balcony beneath the extended eaves. The living spaces and bedrooms face south over the courtyard garden through an ordered elevation of simple casement windows supported on a columnar base. The less formal north elevation, facing onto a quiet street, contains windows to the study, kitchen, and bathrooms. A large window to the stair allows views through the house to the trees behind. This facade composition employs two types of window, made of oak and metal and set at differing depths within the thickness of the masonry wall. Opening louvred vents provide secure night-time ventilation.

Inside, a hierarchy of doors and butterfly-hinged screens enables the living room, dining room and kitchen to be used as discrete entities or opened up to form a single large space. Above the bedrooms on the top floor, a roof-lit studio runs the full length of the house.

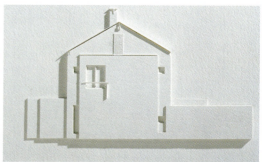
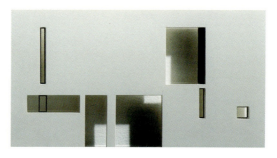
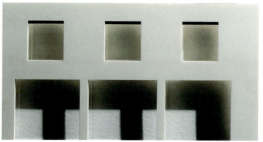

Relief models of the cross section, gable elevation and the entrance and garden facades from inside and outside.

First floor plan

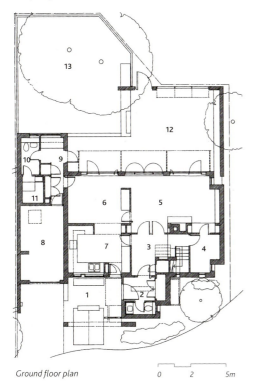

Ground floor plan

0 2 5m

1 *entrance*	**6** *dining*	**11** *sauna*
2 *foyer*	**7** *kitchen*	**12** *terrace*
3 *hall*	**8** *garage*	**13** *lawn*
4 *study*	**9** *utility*	**14** *master bedroom*
5 *living*	**10** *wc and shower*	**15** *bedroom*

STEPHEN BULL'S BISTRO AND BAR
London
1992

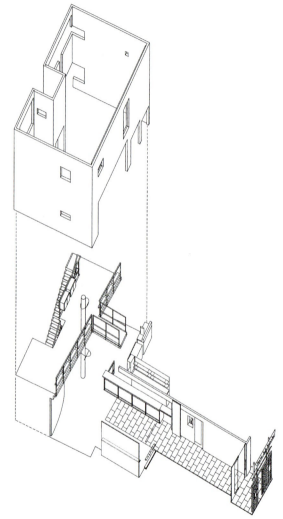

This restaurant occupied a two-storey Victorian warehouse, lit by a single small upper window and accessed by a long passage off St John's Street in Clerkenwell.

The two primary problems – a poorly lit double-height volume and the length of the access passage – generated a creative response. A plaster box with openings the size of windows was inserted within the loosely-defined existing volume so that the resulting interstitial layer, discreetly lit, suggested the presence of indirect daylight. The existing rough structure, painted a deep ox-blood red, was revealed through these new openings, which further provided frames for papier-mâché sculptures that were specially commissioned for the project.

Given the length of the passage, it was possible to provide an extended entrance threshold that felt generous. Behind an elaborate

▲ *Axonometric showing the new plaster 'building within a building'.*
◀ *A metal entrance screen is set within the former shopfront on the street; the bar is aligned on the entrance passageway.*

metal screen and gate, a stone floor, suggesting external space, led to the new restaurant interior. A long bar, placed against one wall of the passage, reduced its apparent length, and provided a distinctive welcome from the street.

The internal details contrasted with the robustness of the principal architectural gestures. An elliptical coat rail emphasised the sole double-height column that supported the mezzanine floor. This was accessed by a simple unwelded steel cantilevered stair. The balustrades, made from painted-steel flats and capped by inclined steamed beech bars, incorporated wooden storage boxes and bent plywood shelves. Strong colours were used on significant planes and one complete upper wall was painted sky blue to enhance the illusion of daylight. The internal fixtures of the restaurant are now lost following a further remodelling.

◀ *An upper gallery overlooks the main space.*
▶ *Cantilevered folded steel stair with timber treads.*

ADMIRAL COURT

Blandford Street, London
1990–92

Blandford Street elevation after and before restoration; ad hoc additions at the back of the houses were demolished.

Admiral Court forms one side of an early-nineteenth-century urban block within a conservation area in Marylebone. During the 1980s a strategy was drawn up that would allow parts of the block to be redeveloped and others to be restored. The centre of the block was largely demolished to allow for the construction of a freestanding office building and the perimeter buildings were restored and returned to a combination of residential, retail and office use.

The proposal for the Blandford Street frontage of the block involved reworking the terrace of eight existing houses. In each case the party walls and facades were retained, together with the rooms that lay behind them, and incorporated into a new development of shops and restaurants at ground and basement level and residences above. Most of the apartments were disposed across two house frontages, forming lateral conversions of the narrow-fronted houses.

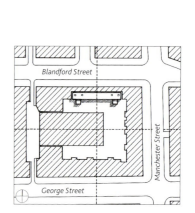

The white-painted render of the new entrance facade reflects light into the courtyard.

The apartments are entered from a new court within the block which is itself accessed by way of a passage formed through one of the original shopfronts. The facade facing the interior of the block, replacing the ad hoc backs of the original houses, is finished in white render with a combination of steel and timber windows to the large and small openings respectively. The rendered facade is treated as a layer which folds forward at each end to enclose the two new stair towers and it is cut away within the plane of the wall to reveal the positions of the original party walls. This serves both to mark the positions of the entrances and to initiate the detail of the coping. The render gives way to Portland stone, suggesting the presence of a discrete layer of ashlar behind the rendered facade.

The distinction between front and back, between street and mews, is reflected in the organisation of the floor plans. The living rooms and bedrooms are located behind the retained facade, recreating both in scale and detail the character of the original Georgian rooms, while the kitchens, bathrooms and second bedrooms face south onto the court. On the top floor the orientation of the plans is reconfigured to allow the living rooms to face south through the horizontal glazing of the attic storey.

◀ The rendered surface is cut back to reveal Portland stone both at the cornice level on the line of original party walls, and adjacent to the entrance.
▶ Metal entrance gates give access to a passageway, formed within the smallest of the former shop fronts, which leads through to the inner courtyard.

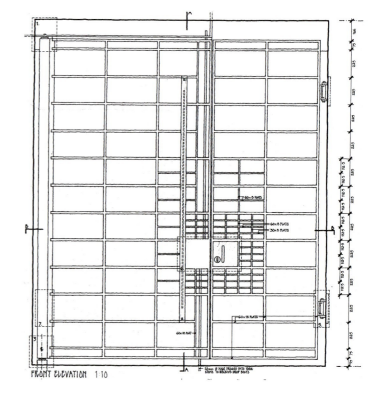

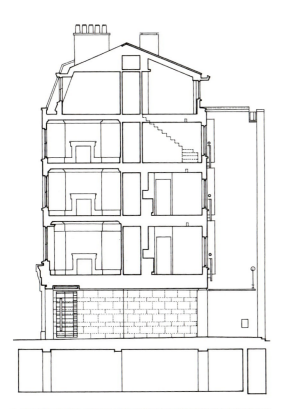

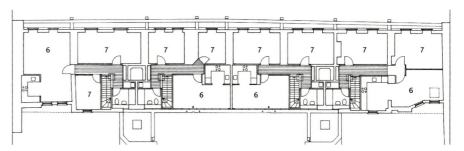

Fourth floor plan

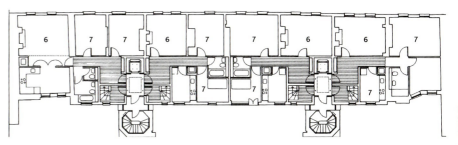

Third floor plan

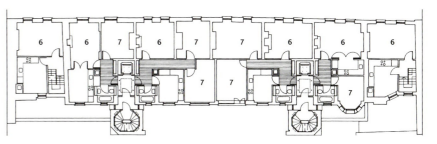

First floor plan

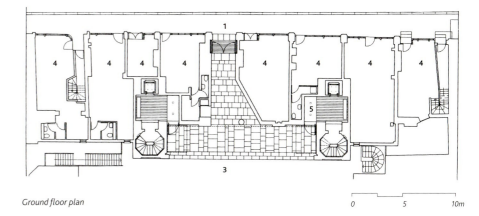

Ground floor plan

1 *street entrance*
2 *passage*
3 *courtyard*
4 *shops*
5 *entrance lobby*
6 *living room*
7 *bedroom/study*

NATIONAL MUSEUM OF CONTEMPORARY ART

Helsinki

1993

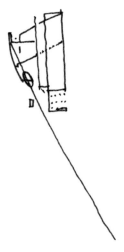

Conditions of anonymity for entrants to the competition for the National Museum of Contemporary Art in Helsinki led Allies and Morrison to select the codename Cothurnocystis. This unusual primitive marine organism has its internal organs asymmetrically disposed within its body – the result, scientists believe, of resting on the seabed on its side. Likewise the competition design was conceived as an organism whose internal structure appears to have evolved in response to a series of entirely extraneous factors.

The simple rectangular gallery spaces are threaded through by a more complex armature which contains the various public facilities and whose form responds both to the detailed requirements of the brief and the particular geometries and relationships of the site. So the orthogonal form of the galleries – rationally determined by the discipline of the interior – gives way to the curving line of the external wall to the courtyard, which in turn follows the gentle alignment of the main road.

The site for the new museum was a triangular piece of land between Eliel Saarinen's railway station to the east, the neoclassical town hall to the west and Alvar Aalto's Finlandia Hall

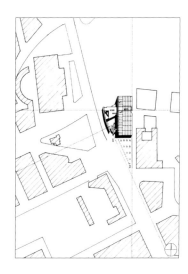

Model showing the three principal elements of the proposal: the gallery space, the more complex 'servant' building, and the enclosed south-facing courtyard.

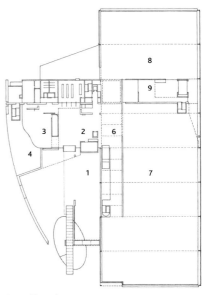

Ground floor plan

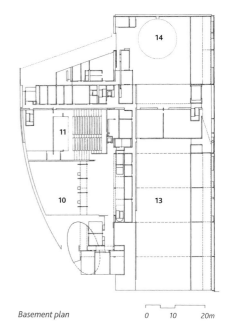

1 entrance court
2 foyer
3 cafe
4 terrace
5 shop
6 gallery foyer
7 permanent display
8 temporary exhibition
9 workshop
10 paper art and video
11 auditorium
12 education
13 storage
14 goods/servicing

Basement plan

0   10   20m

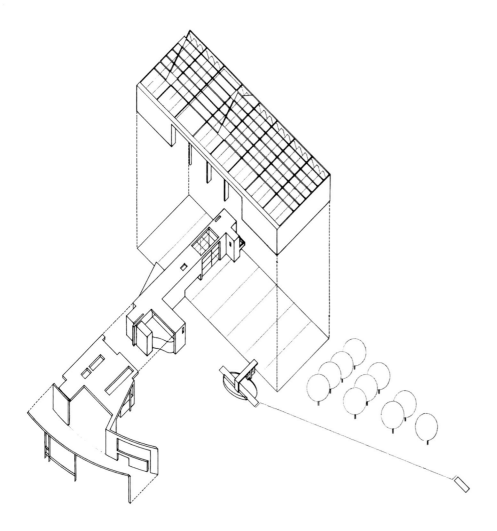

to the north. The public entrance to the new museum was to be located on the southern boundary of the site and approached through a new landscaped square. However, the main facade of the building was to face Mannerheimintie to the west, allowing the museum to take its place among the major public buildings that address this important route into the city. Accordingly, the facade to Mannerheimintie comprised a long and gently curving wall, pierced to reveal the entrance courtyard to the museum, the cafe with its terrace and, in the distance, the main enclosure of the exhibition spaces. The configuration of the wall was a response both to the adjustment in the alignment of the street and to the orientation of the town hall, and as such contrasted with the galleries whose orthogonal geometry was extrapolated from the main urban grid. A formal distinction was also made between the galleries and ancillary accommodation.

While the entrance and ancillary areas were defined and specific, the galleries had a need for flexibility and an obligation to avoid being overly formal or precious. They were therefore designed as a series of undivided top-lit loft-like spaces. The contrasting nature of the spaces was reflected in their construction – the galleries had a steel-framed structure with metal panel cladding, while the entrance and ancillary spaces were reinforced concrete faced in granite and white-painted stucco.

The principal entrance route from Mannerheimintie crosses a bridge over an elliptical lightwell to the basement, passing the gallery building to the right.

SOUTHBANK CENTRE
People's Palace
1994

As part of a wide-ranging commission that ran from the mid-1990s, Allies and Morrison completed six projects within the Royal Festival Hall: the restoration of the foyer spaces, the Hothouse, the Gamelan Room, the People's Palace restaurant, and two new ground-floor cafes. The restored foyer spaces were a first step in the recovery of the original architectural plan with its high- and low-level entrances. This project (1994) was made possible by moving the education facility from the double-height space of the foyer to an area under the side terrace, released by the removal of redundant plant. Here, the new Hothouse with a sprung floor and support facilities was inserted into the existing bare concrete shell. The Gamelan Room was installed in similar storage space under the ballroom floor.

On the first floor the People's Palace restaurant was reinstated in the same location as the long gone 1951 Festival of Britain restaurant, taking full advantage of the double-height 36-metre-long river frontage. The principal intervention is a single plaster armature that springs from the rear wall of the restaurant where it attaches to the existing core, framing two tall entrance doors at each side. Arranged symmetrically on the axis of the auditorium, the armature rises to form a canopy that fans out to embrace the volume of the room and the river views beyond. The restaurant was refurbished as part of the later major restoration of the Royal Festival Hall, and reopened as the Skylon, in honour of the celebrated temporary structure from the Festival of Britain.

On the ground floor two further cafes were added, Café 51 (1994), facing Queen's Walk, and the Festival Café (2003), facing Belvedere Road.

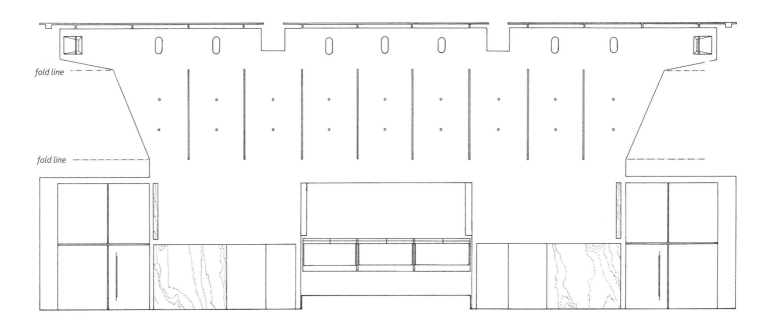

The plaster armature (shown 'unfolded' in the drawing) frames the entrance doors and folds up to meet the facade column of the original 1951 enclosure.

Further major works were planned at this stage, including the reconfiguration and restoration of the auditorium and foyers, a new building running alongside and screening Hungerford Bridge, housing shops at terrace level with administration for the arts centre above, and a new under-terrace development, replacing Café 51 and facing Queen's Walk.

The overall scheme was intended to provide all the necessary technical improvements and integrates the Royal Festival Hall into both the urban topography and the fabric of the existing city.

▲ The bar is set on a raised platform.
▶ Detail of armature.

SOUTHBANK CENTRE
Temporary Installations
1994

As part of its involvement at the Southbank Centre, Allies and Morrison carried out a number of commissions for temporary installations. Two of these in particular required considerable ingenuity within a limited budget.

The imposition of new insurance restrictions that limited the serving of food and drink in proximity to works of art forced the Hayward Gallery to find a new space for its receptions. While a long-term solution was required, provision was needed for the immediate season and, with limited space available within the gallery, use was made of one of the large external terraces.

The pavilion's structure of red-oxide painted sawn softwood derived from the module of uncut 2.4 by 1.2 metre timber boards. Three four-metre-high double columns, partially wrapped in grey rope, supported a simple matrix of joists, spaced to hide the joints between the panels to give the illusion of a single honey-coloured surface folded over the ends and the top of the structural network. Cantilevered arms extended from the columns to support plywood plates onto which industrial uplighters were mounted. The open face of the resultant portal was enclosed with a series of standard doors, doubled to form four-metre-high openings, allowing the whole wall to open to a decked terrace in summer.

The pavilion, constructed in one month and intended to last only two seasons, survived intensive use for five years before being dismantled in 2003.

The second project involved the reuse of an existing plant room beneath the Hungerford Terrace on the west side of the Royal Festival Hall. Space was needed for new music education activities, such as interactive workshops, and use was made of a redundant air-conditioning plant room, hence the nickname The Hothouse. The new multi-functional facility can also be used for dance rehearsals.

The Education Room was inserted within the concrete shell of the former plant room.

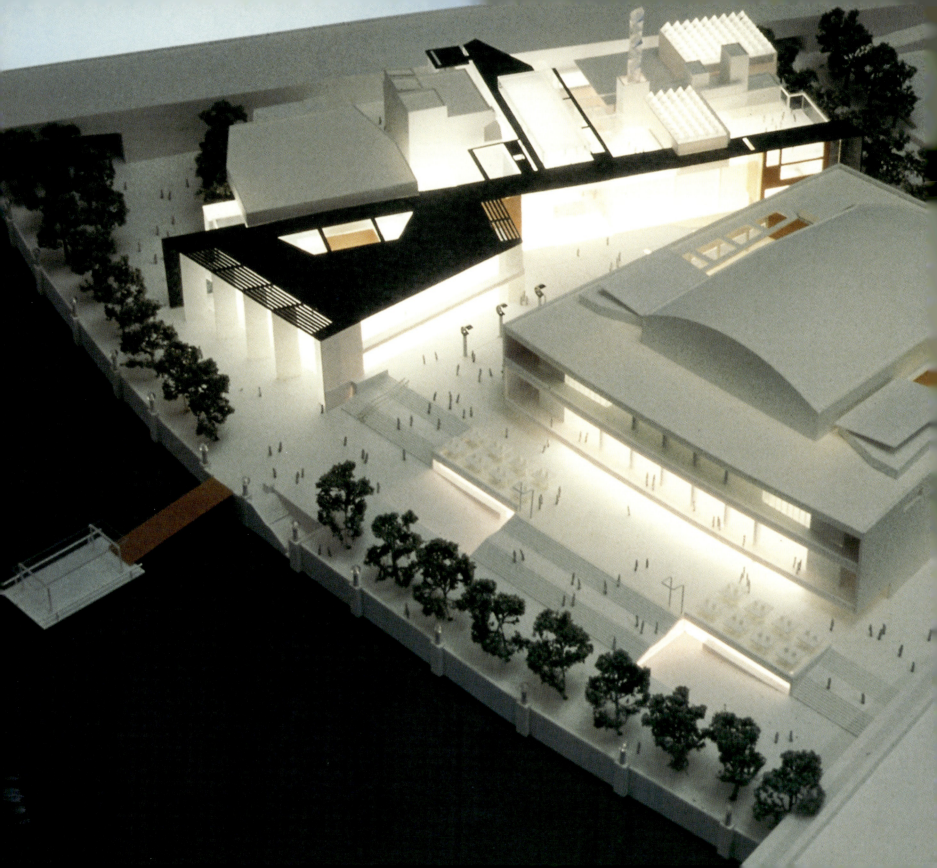

SOUTHBANK CENTRE
Masterplan
1994–2003

A legacy of the 1951 Festival of Britain, the Royal Festival Hall is today regarded as one of the major British buildings of its time. As the South Bank arts centre was developed, the concert hall came to be surrounded by a series of buildings, some more distinguished than others, but many of the spaces between them were either neglected, mistreated or subjected to experimental or temporary interventions. In addition, various proposals to bring some coherence to the site, ranging from the commercial infilling of its yawning gaps to its subjugation by a greater order, have all met with political indecision or lack of funding. As a result, the arts centre remained disconnected from its immediate urban fabric.

In 1994 an invited international competition was held for a new masterplan for the South Bank arts centre, with the prospect of funding from the newly instigated National Lottery. The objectives of Allies and Morrison's proposal (placed second) were to integrate the arts centre with the surrounding city, provide a strong sense of unity for its facilities, and develop the full potential of all the existing buildings on the site. Above all, the proposal was based on the inherited realities of the site rather than arbitrarily imposing a new order.

To some extent, the task of the masterplan was to remove a number of the interventions that had been made over the years. The 1964 extension to the Royal Festival Hall, while well crafted, had reoriented the building to face the river, diminishing its connection with Belvedere Road and undermining the internal circulation of the building that so elegantly resolved the pre-existing difference in levels. The addition of a series of concrete walkways, as part of the Hayward Gallery and Queen Elizabeth Hall development, further isolated the Royal Festival Hall from its surroundings, adding confusion and relegating the street level to a

▲ The Royal Festival Hall in 1994.
◀ Model showing the proposed extension to the Hayward Gallery on the left and the Thames-side steps to Royal Festival Hall on the right.

The proposed extension to the Hayward Gallery helped to redefine the public space on the south side of the Royal Festival Hall.

1 Hungerford Bridge
2 pedestrian route to Charing Cross station
3 upper entrance to Royal Festival Hall
4 Royal Festival Hall auditorium
5 lower entrance to Royal Festival Hall
6 piazza
7 lower entrance to Queen Elizabeth Hall and Hayward Gallery
8 new gallery
9 Hayward Gallery foyer
10 workshop
11 Museum of the Moving Image entrance
12 Waterloo Bridge

labyrinth of service entrances and storage areas. The legacy of the 1964 interventions, however, was a group of four buildings, all with public foyers at first-floor level.

But, rather than working against this defining characteristic, Allies and Morrison's proposal replaced the walkways with a single uninterrupted pedestrian podium or piano nobile, fully occupying the space between the buildings. Approached by generous staircases from both Belvedere Road on the south side and the new riverside Queen's Walk on the north, the podium would allow direct connections between the buildings for the first time, linking with the cross-river pedestrian traffic from the upper levels of Waterloo and Hungerford Bridges. This podium would become the focus of the arts centre – a new heart, overlooked by all the buildings, and a raised open-air vestibule with spectacular views of the Thames. At ground level, a roof-lit foyer would give access to each of the buildings and create a single main entrance to the arts centre from Belvedere Road.

The operation of the Hayward Gallery would be transformed by a new two-storey armature located between the gallery and the Queen Elizabeth Hall. With a second entrance on Waterloo Bridge, this new foyer space, containing a shop and a cafe, would connect to a new restaurant on the roof of the Queen Elizabeth Hall, leading to terraces with panoramic views across the river.

The foyer of the Queen Elizabeth Hall, internalised by its impenetrable layer of toilets and cloakrooms, would be replanned. The support spaces would be relocated in the part of the unused floor below, releasing the perimeters of both floors to engage with the outside.

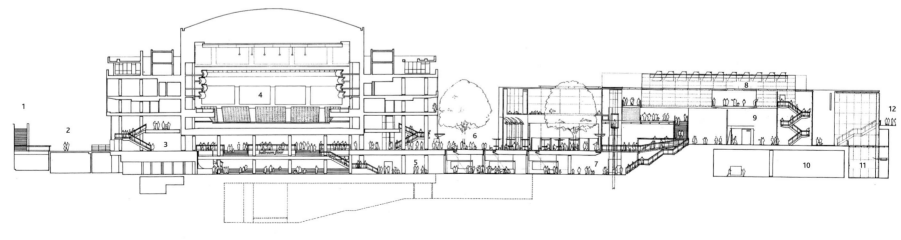

Royal Festival Hall   new square   Hayward Gallery

SARUM HALL SCHOOL
London
1991–95

The new building for this small private girls' school is located on the south side of Eton Avenue, an exceptional street of late-nineteenth-century Queen Anne Revival houses in Belsize Park. The character of the street is determined by the palette of materials – brick, slate, tile and render – and the vocabulary of forms arising from the traditional construction of load-bearing walls and pitched roofs. Particular interest, however, arises from the elevational variety and the diversity of elements brought together within a single house as entrances, staircases, north-light windows and projecting dormers are disposed in close juxtaposition.

◀ *The entrance canopy links the building with the street and provides a protected area at the entrance to the school.*
▶ *View from the street through the main hall to the playground beyond.*

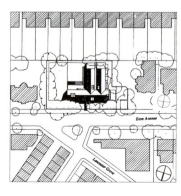

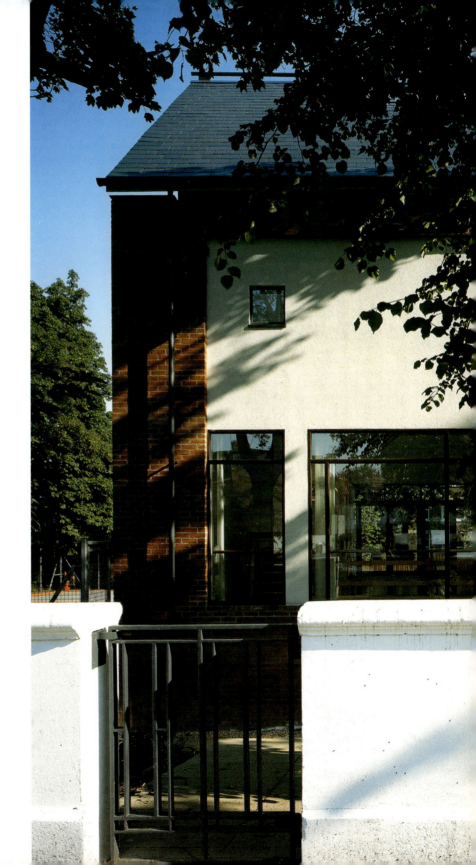

1 *entrance court*
2 *entrance hall*
3 *offices*
4 *school hall/gymnasium*
5 *dining room*
6 *kitchen*
7 *music room*
8 *classroom*
9 *playground*
10 *tennis court*
11 *art room*
12 *science room*
13 *void over hall*
14 *library*

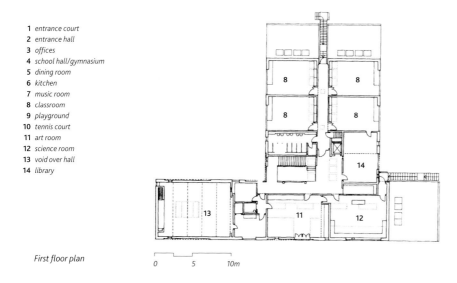

First floor plan

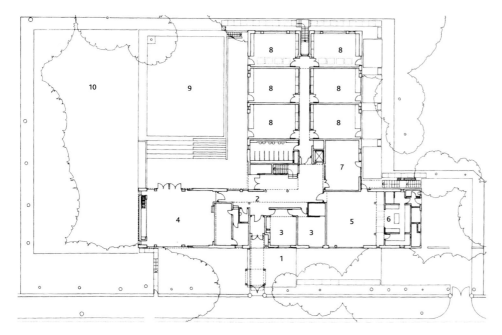

Ground floor plan

The new building, like the late-Victorian house which the school previously occupied, is organised around an open staircase with all the main spaces of the school – hall, dining room, library, head teacher's office and classroom corridors – leading from it. While the repetitive elements of the classrooms are placed to the rear of the site, the more individual spaces – hall, dining room, science and art rooms – are located along the street frontage and articulated in response to their use, producing an appropriately rich and varied elevation to the street. Here too the main entrance, like those of the neighbouring houses, has a porch, canopy and gateposts to the street.

The planar roof is set above the layered external walls of brick and render. The significant change in level across the site made it possible to provide a south-facing terrace of steps.

South elevation

North elevation

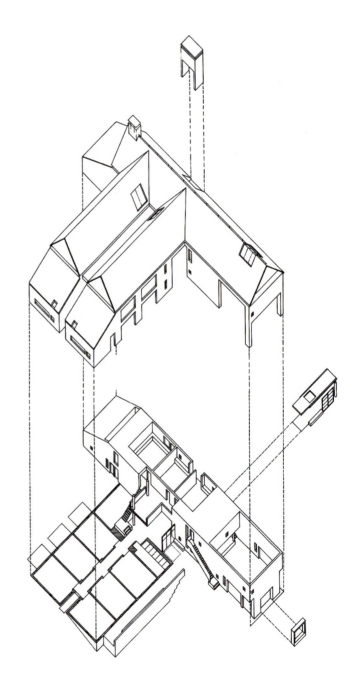

▲ The north-facing dormer window lights the art room and signals the school entrance below.

◀ Entrance hall and staircase.

The walls of handmade red brick, punctuated by recessed panels of white render, form an inner layer that expresses the main interior spaces. The pitched slate roof is articulated by fine detailing to the gables, eaves and ridge. Incisions in the roof accommodate elements such as the north light to the art room, the lantern to the gymnasium, and the chimney. The windows, which vary considerably in size, are framed in a combination of hardwood and metal and are set flush with the plane of the white render.

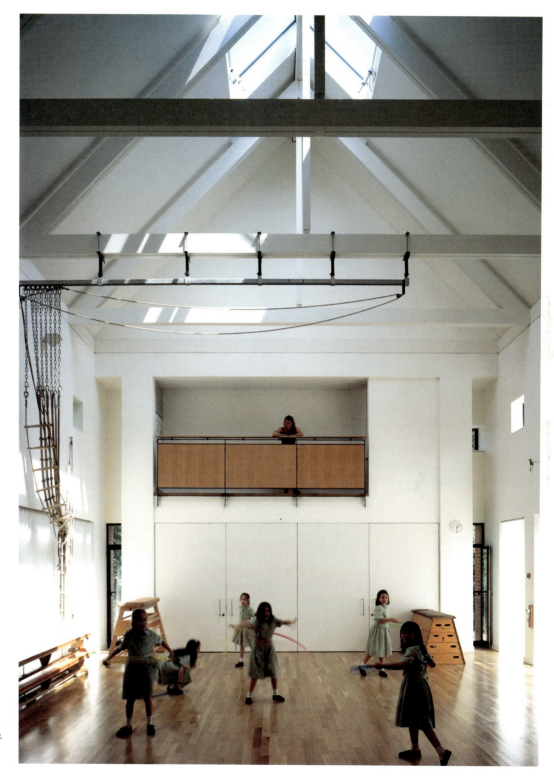

The multi-purpose main hall, lit from both sides and above, is overlooked by gallery at first-floor level.

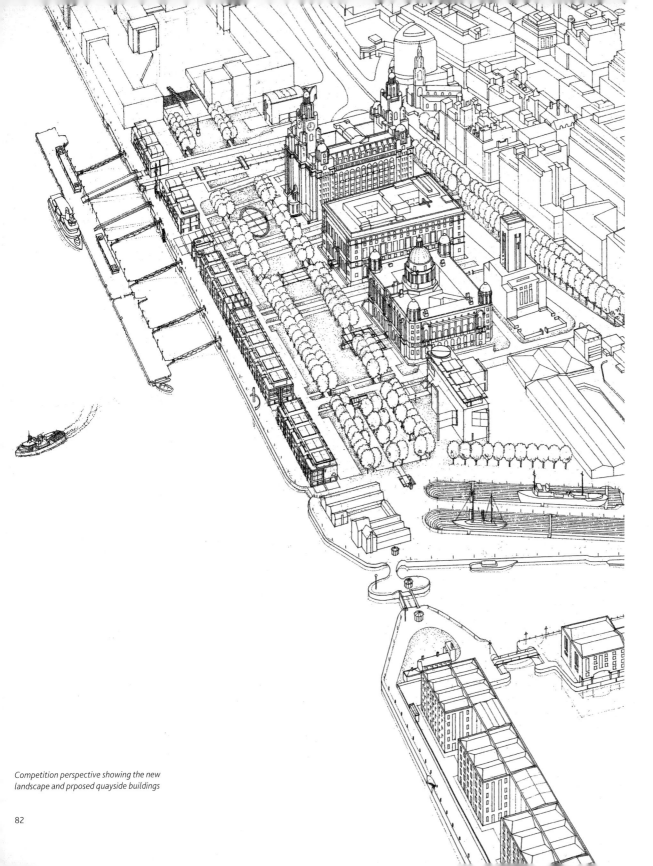

Competition perspective showing the new landscape and prposed quayside buildings

PIERHEAD
Liverpool
1990–95

It would be hard to exaggerate the importance of the Pierhead to the city of Liverpool. Constructed on an area of landfill within the broad band of the docks, it provides a physical and symbolic bridgehead between the commercial centre of the city and the River Mersey. The 'Three Graces', the great Edwardian buildings that define the site, have come to stand as symbols of Liverpool's maritime tradition and the prosperity it created.

Historically, however, the space in front of the three buildings has never fully matched their grandeur. A flat-roofed bus station constructed in the 1960s obstructed views from and to the river and the remainder of the site was used as a bus park. Although the Pierhead remained a popular meeting place, partly because of its history as an embarkation point for transatlantic liners, the Mersey ferry terminal provided the only remaining clue to its maritime past.

The site not only turned its back on the Mersey, but it had no effective pedestrian connections with either the city's commercial centre to the east or the restored Albert Dock complex to the south. The riverside walk had been extended as far as the Pierhead but here its granite setts abruptly gave way to broken concrete paving and tarmac. At its northern end the site was bounded by the 'floating roadway', a walled tidal inlet of the Mersey that formed a visual and physical barrier.

The development of the Pierhead, in parallel with a major programme of renewal in the docks including the

Aerial view before redevelopment.

The landscape plan connects with the city grid.

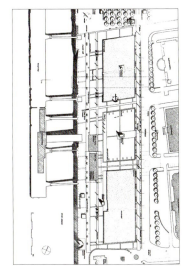
Proposed landscape plan.

Maritime Museum and Tate Liverpool, offered an opportunity to re-establish the significance of the site. Reorganised as a major civic space, the Pierhead now forms not only an appropriate setting for the Three Graces, but also a focus for all the new amenities assembled along the waterfront to the south and a stimulus to the restoration and regeneration of the dockland areas to the north.

The new landscape links the city to the river, and Albert Dock to Princes Dock, with a new urban park. In the centre of the park, in front of the Cunard Building, is a paved square, facilitating pedestrian circulation to and from the ferry terminal and providing a site for public events and gatherings. In front of the three landmark buildings an avenue of trees marks the edge of the park, while a footpath extends from the entrance of the Maritime Museum to the floating roadway. A new footbridge nearer the waterfront permits a similar northwards extension of the existing riverside walkway.

The smooth landscaped surface has facilitated access which had been denied wherever setts were used elsewhere on the waterfront. New streetlights, benches, shelters and litter bins were specially designed for the site. The existing statues and monuments were retained and restored, while the new park provided an appropriate setting for the introduction of further pieces, the first of which was a circular bandstand dedicated to those who lost their lives in the supply convoys of the Second World War.

BRITISH EMBASSY
Dublin
1992–95

The new British Embassy in the Irish capital is designed as a series of interconnecting buildings grouped around an inner courtyard. This cloister-like space provides a central focus for the activities of the embassy in an arrangement that recalls the typology of many of Dublin's major public buildings. The public entrance to the embassy is on Merrion Road and a separate staff and service entrance is provided at the rear via a shared access. The plan allows the reception and security desk to directly oversee the public entrance and, through the courtyard, the private entrance. Embassy staff and their visitors then pass through a double-height hall overlooking the central courtyard.

The composition of the three-storey facade on Merrion Road establishes a distinction between the main entrance to the embassy, positioned centrally in the formal stone-faced, five-bay elevation, and a less formal

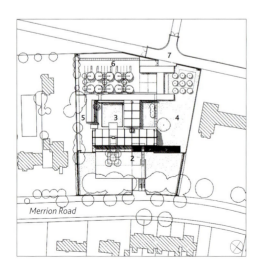

1 *gatehouse*
2 *forecourt*
3 *courtyard*
4 *garden*
5 *VIP parking*
6 *staff parking*
7 *service entrance*

The omission of the granite face to reveal the metal layer behind signals the public importance of the consular entrance.

The courtyard facade is recessed at ground level to incorporate direct access for staff.

entrance for consular enquiries. The internal organisation of the embassy is represented in the tripartite division into base, piano nobile and attic storey. The facade is faced in Wicklow granite and is articulated further by a trabeated metal grid that supports the slate roof. The courtyard buildings are constructed of red brick, corresponding both to the adjacent Thomas Prior House and to neighbouring domestic properties.

At piano nobile level, each bay of the principal facade contains a large window positioned centrally within the structural grid. Here the external layer of granite is 'removed' to reveal a metal surface within which the window frame sits. The windows are further subdivided to provide a fixed panel of narrow ventilation grilles behind which are manually operated internal shutters. The vents, which remain secure and waterproof even when fully open, allow cross-ventilation to be achieved across the comparatively narrow eight-metre-wide floor width. On summer nights they can be left open to cool the concrete structure, thereby helping to reduce the daytime cooling load.

The landscape is planned so as to establish an appropriately formal public forecourt at the front of the

View from main courtyard looking back towards the staff entrance.

Gate to courtyard from the car park.

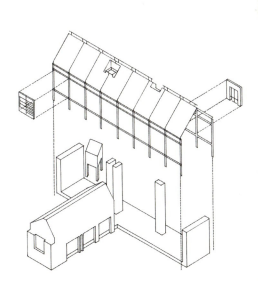

Detail of facade to the consular section.

Ambassador's entrance.

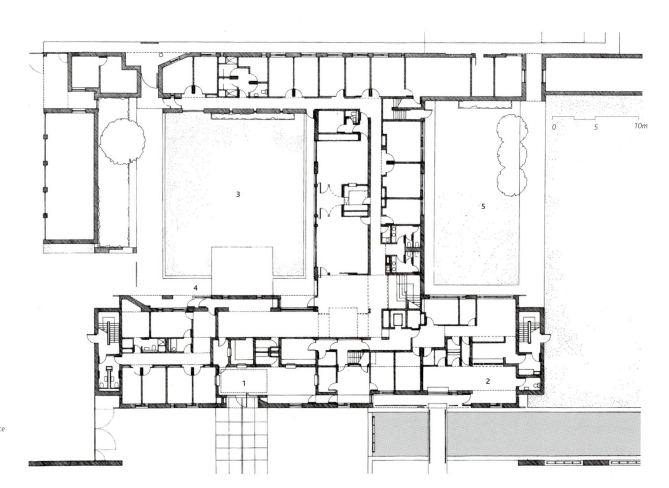

1 *main entrance*
2 *consular entrance*
3 *courtyard*
4 *staff entrance*
5 *garden*

Oblique view of the facade from the west. A bridge crosses the linear pool to provide access to the entrance to the consular section.

North elevation facing Merrion Road

East elevation and section through car park and courtyard

embassy and a relaxed series of garden spaces towards the rear of the site. This is articulated by a manipulation of the ground levels, and organised in plan within a framework generated from the setting out of the elevations. The building appears to stand on a continuous plane of Portland stone that, like the facades, is stripped back, but here to reveal grass, water, gravel or planting.

The double-height space providing access to the main meeting room is overlooked by the first-floor circulation routes.

NUNNERY SQUARE
Sheffield
1993–95

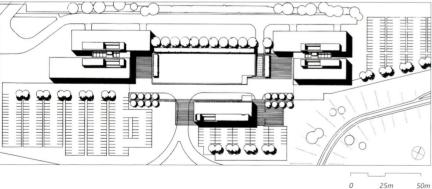

This building was constructed as the first phase of a new business park on a redundant railway site a short distance from the centre of Sheffield. A group of three buildings was planned not around a car park, as often seems the case, but centred on a rectangular lawn, the fourth side of which was defined by a screen of pleached limes and a row of horse chestnut trees.

Each of the buildings was sited so that its entrance related directly to the central landscape and visitors arrive from this side. Car parking was placed at the edges of the site, away from the central space.

The first building was the smallest and the most straightforward and, in the event, the only phase to be completed by Allies and Morrison. Its simple rectangular plan is enclosed by a skin of cladding that responds to the 1.5-metre internal planning module, the 9-metre structural grid, and the floor levels. Set forward from

The outer layer of the facade is omitted at the corner, establishing a larger scale and a stronger spatial relationship between the building and its site at the entrance.

Construction view

this primary volume stands a white trabeated metal frame that, at a practical level, provides support for brises-soleil and access for window cleaning. The juxtaposition of scales between this and the inner envelope also provided the means to articulate the entrances, to establish a presence on the site, and to contribute to the definition of the external spaces.

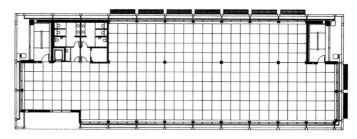
Typical upper floor plan

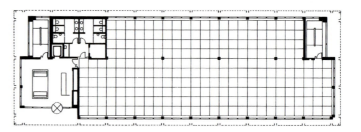
Ground floor plan

ROSALIND FRANKLIN BUILDING
NEWNHAM COLLEGE
Cambridge
1993–95

This project, which provides new postgraduate student accommodation for the college, consists of a simple, linear building following the eastern boundary of the site. In this way, the new building emulates the organisation of the existing college buildings – where a continuous perimeter block encompasses private gardens at the centre – as well as forming the enclosure to a new garden setting for a 1970s hall of residence, the Strachey Building. While the building may be approached internally from the new graduate garden, the external entrances are from a semi-private lane that connects Sidgwick Avenue to Newnham Walk. In this way a balance has been achieved between integrating the new building with the main college, and allowing the graduate students a degree of independence. At night the lane and the entrance undercrofts can be secured by gates.

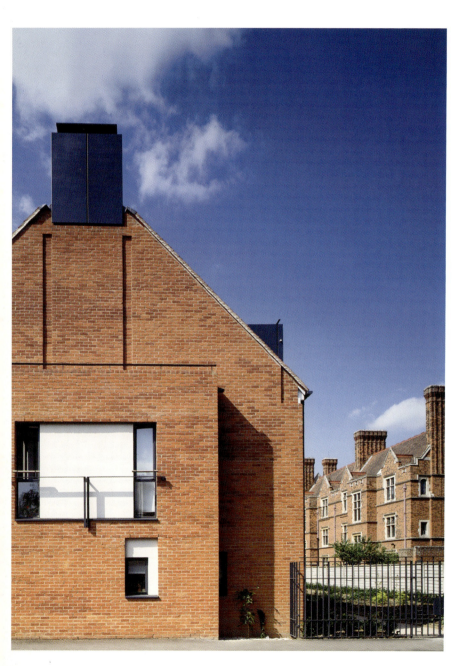
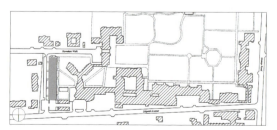

◀ *South gable*
▶ *West-facing garden facade*

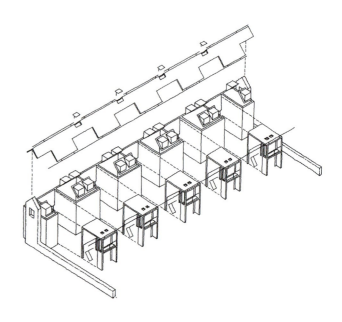

The disposition of the building also helps to define the two main college entrances, from Sidgwick Avenue and Newnham Walk, and the two external spaces that preface the visitor's arrival at the college. The southern gable of the new building and the wall and railings that secure the southern boundary of the graduate garden provide the necessary containment to the approach from Newnham Walk, while on Sidgwick Avenue a clear hierarchy of external spaces provides a new structure to the threshold to the College. The entrance forecourt is more contained, focusing directly on the porter's lodge and opening up a view of the lodge from Sidgwick Avenue, and given more definition by the introduction of new granite sett paving, by the relocation of the existing gate to the Sidgwick Avenue frontage and the addition of a planted screen to the face of the porter's lodge.

◄ *White-painted timber balconies separate the 'villas' and overlook the garden.*
► *The entrances from the 'lane' punctuate the otherwise continuous wall.*

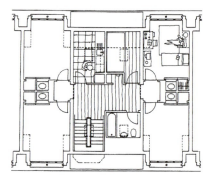

Second floor plan: student house

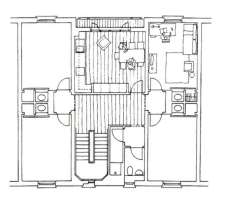

First floor plan: student house

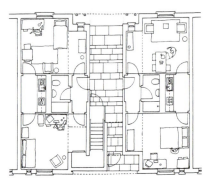

Ground floor plan: one-bedroom flat

The long, pitched-roof building is itself divided into five units, each containing two one-bedroom flats and a student 'house' comprising eight study-bedrooms, common room, laundry, two bathrooms and storeroom. The one-bedroom flats are located at ground level, with the student house arranged above at first and second floor levels.

Front doors to both the flats and the student houses are located at ground level within a passage or undercroft, which also provides a private link to the graduate garden; the students in the ground-floor flats can either participate in the life of the student house above them or remain independent. Two rooms situated at ground level are designed for disabled occupancy.

While the plan of the student rooms is arranged symmetrically about the central axis of the building, the articulation of the rooms on the east and west elevations is expressed very differently. Where the building faces the lane, the facade reads as a continuous two-storey wall pierced only at ground level at the entrances to the cross passages, and – within the roof – by dormer windows related to each study bedroom. In contrast, where the building faces the graduate garden, the continuity of the wall is broken and the accommodation is articulated instead as a series of discrete brick pavilions containing study bedrooms, alternating with the white-painted timber screens of the kitchen/dining rooms. Above the brick pavilions rise the dormers,

The mature landscape photographed in 2006.

East elevation

West elevation

Beneath the single roof the facades are organised so as to present an open western aspect to the garden and the college, and a more secure eastern aspect to the town. The centre line of the 'villas' is signalled by 'chimneys' which collect all the service outlets.

grouped in pairs to emphasise the verticality of the individual pavilions.

This difference between the two elevations acknowledges the distinction between the public world of the lane and the private world of the garden, between outside and inside, between back and front, in the same manner as Basil Champneys' original college buildings. What is restrained and small-scale on the outer elevation is rendered more expansive and flamboyant on the inner elevation, creating an appropriate backdrop to the landscaped garden.

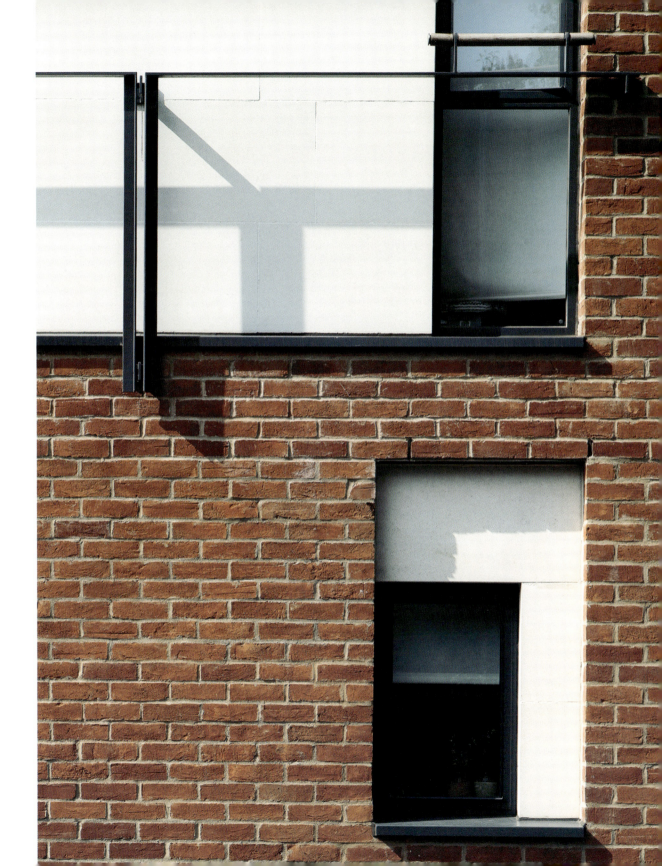

STUDENT UNION SHOP
University of Southampton
1993–95

Sited at the heart of university campus designed in the 1960s by Basil Spence, this new pavilion provides additional retail facilities for the adjacent student union. The form and location of the building responds to the principles of Spence's original plan in which freestanding, orthogonally planned buildings were placed within the informal landscape and dramatic topography of the site.

A double-height portico exaggerates the scale of this modest building and helps to frame a sheltered meeting space outside the entrance to the student union. The long brick facade reinforces the southern boundary of the university's central green. While the ground floor on this elevation contains no windows (the supermarket didn't require them), the upper floor is punctuated by three large openings with shutters that can fold out to allow ventilation of the top-floor linear gallery. This gallery provides a common access route to three separate lettable units. Roof-lit throughout its length, it is envisaged as a type of public space and acts as a thermal buffer to the single glazing of the retail units.

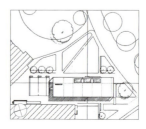

1 portico
2 student union shop
3 gallery
4 shop
5 office

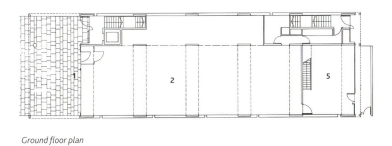

Ground floor plan

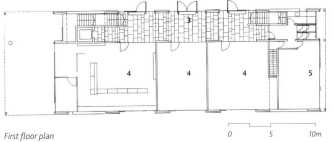

First floor plan

0 5 10m

REGENT STREET MASTERPLAN
London
1995

1 *retained Regent Street facade*
2 *arcade*
3 *office*
4 *public square*
5 *hotel*
6 *residential*

Aerial view from north and model view from south.

Regent Street forms part of the major urban intervention made by John Nash in the early nineteenth century in which the gardens of St James's Park were linked with the new landscape of Regent's Park, creating a new north-south thoroughfare and a setting for a significant residential expansion of the city.

The sweeping curve of the southern part of Regent Street, rebuilt in the 1920s, was regarded as an elegant if pragmatic response to the constraints of land ownership. In fact the conflict between the alignment of the new street and the surrounding urban structure has always been problematic, compromising the continuity of the east-west streets, creating inappropriately shallow building depths (relative to the frontages), and giving rise to a confusing configuration of service streets and building backs.

Allies and Morrison's masterplan for the south-east sector of the street addressed these problems by proposing a radical reorganisation of the buildings on Regent Street and the redevelopment of the site of the Regent Palace Hotel immediately to the east. Fundamental to the scheme was a new arcade following the line of the existing Glasshouse Street. This gave new significance and value to a hitherto neglected part of the site, drawing the life of Regent Street through to the interior of the block and creating a new pedestrian route from Piccadilly Circus.

The need to phase the construction led to a division of the site into six discrete development plots, combining new construction with restoration and reconstruction. Behind the retained facade of Regent Street, two new five-storey office buildings were proposed, each with a central atrium at first-floor level. Ground and mezzanine floors were intended for retail use, with additional retail, storage and servicing at basement levels. Between the office buildings, an existing retail arcade was retained and reconfigured.

A block to the east of the Regent Street crescent was to be occupied by retail at ground level and a 200-bedroom hotel above, with the reception and public spaces opening onto an atrium at mezzanine level. The entrance to the hotel faced a new small square at the north-west corner of the site while the south end of the site near Piccadilly Circus provided public access to a leisure and entertainment complex at basement level. An adjacent site on Brewer Street was intended for residential and retail use. By concentrating the large-scale office and retail uses on the major streets and placing the hotel, and smaller-scale residential and retail uses on the secondary streets, the masterplan established a hierarchy of scale that was sympathetic to the existing context.

The proposed top-lit arcade aligns with Glasshouse Street.

CONTEMPORARY APPLIED ARTS
London
1995–96

This independent gallery exhibits contemporary ceramics, jewellery, textiles, furniture, metalwork and glass in the ground and basement floors of an eighteenth-century building on Percy Street in London's Fitzrovia. A nineteenth-century top-lit extension, accessible from a rear mews, occupied the back of the site. Allies and Morrison's brief called for a flexible space that could accommodate temporary solo or group exhibitions, a gallery/shop for showing and selling the work of Contemporary Applied Arts' 250 members and a meeting room and staff offices.

On entering the gallery, visitors find themselves in a single space that extends to the full depth of the site and down into the basement. By opening up a double-height space between the two floors in the centre of the plan, deep sightlines are established from the fully glazed shopfront to the back of the site on both levels, and a space is created for the display of large objects or hangings.

◀ *The upper and lower exhibition spaces are visible through the glazed shopfront.*
▶ *Axonometric view showing composition of the central space.*

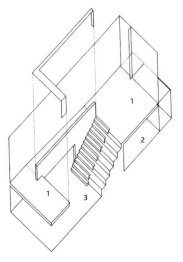

1 *gallery*
2 *meeting room*
3 *shop*

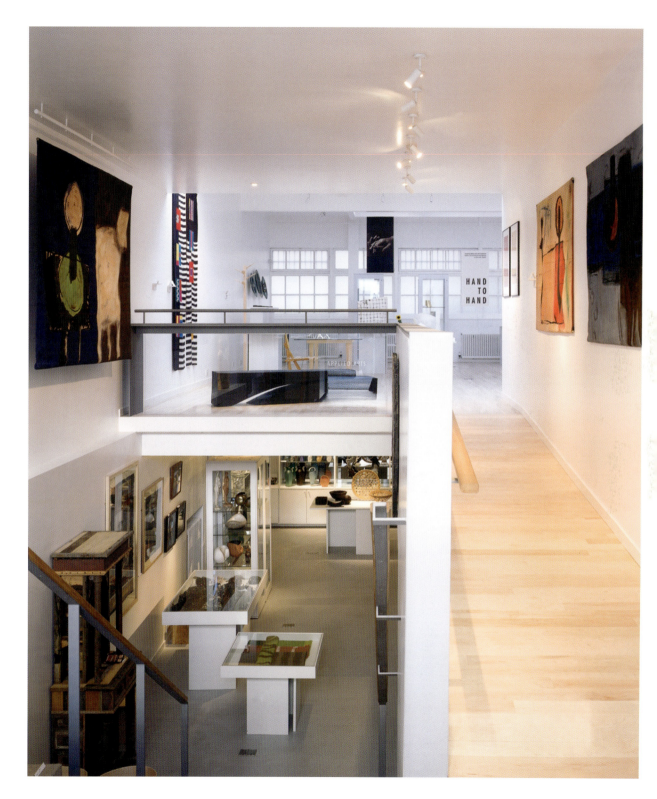

From the front reception area a shallow ramp leads up to the top-lit main exhibition space and a wide in situ concrete staircase leads down to the basement shop, lined with wall units for the display of smaller objects. Between the ramp and the stair in this central void is a free-standing wall, the top of which sets a horizontal datum, with a steel capping that extends to provide a 'floating' display shelf above the glass balustrade to the exhibition space.

The internal finishes are simple and direct, providing an appropriate background for the objects on display. Walls and ceilings are white-painted plasterboard, floors are maple, resin and exposed concrete and balustrades are steel and glass.

In situ concrete staircase with steel balustrade and timber rail.

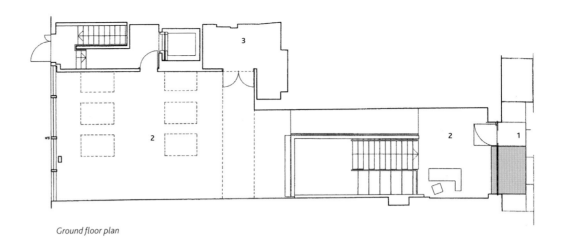

Ground floor plan

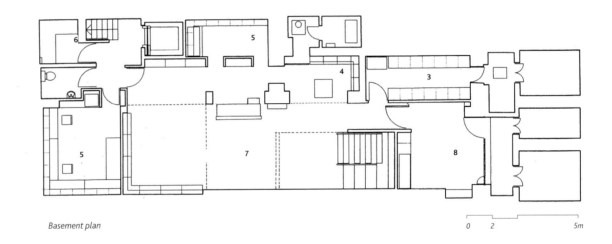

Basement plan

0 2 5m

1 *main entrance*
2 *gallery*
3 *store*
4 *jewellery*
5 *office*
6 *kitchen*
7 *shop*
8 *meeting room*

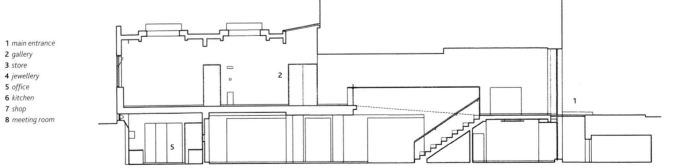

Section

ABBEY MILLS PUMPING STATION
London
1994–97

Commissioned by Thames Water as part of its renewal of the sewage pumping complex at Abbey Mills in east London, the new pumping station is sited in a meadow adjacent to several existing pump houses. Its purpose is to raise by 12 metres the level of incoming sewage, gravitating from a large area of inner London, so that it can continue on its route to a processing plant at Beckton four miles further east.

The above-ground structure, designed by Allies and Morrison, is matched below ground by a concrete substructure of equal volume where the sewage enters the building. Pumps raise the sewage to channels at ground level, where it continues in a parallel route, exiting from the opposite end. This operational logic determines both the linear and symmetrical nature of the building.

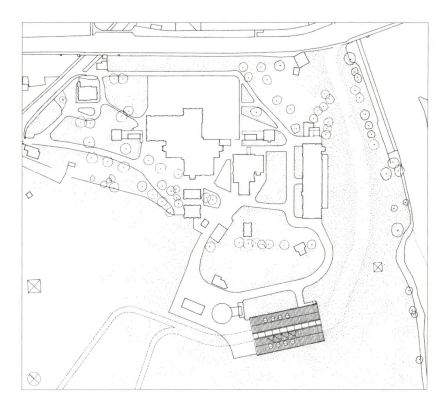

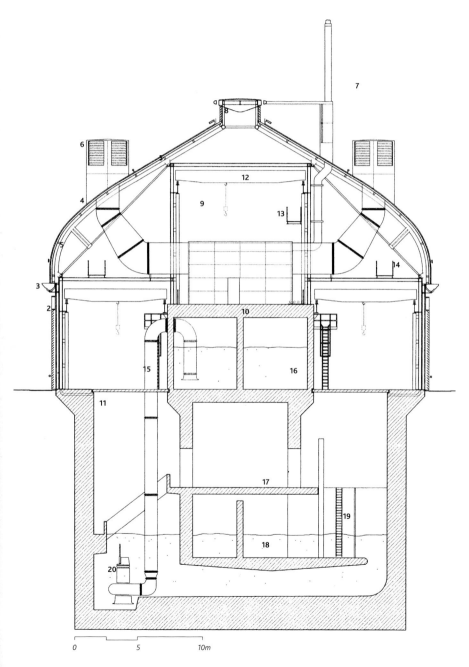

The arrangement of the building above ground arises from two principal requirements: first, that the new building, like its Victorian predecessors, should be self-sufficient in terms of its energy needs, and second, that all of the mechanical components can be easily replaced if necessary. Thus four diesel generators power the pumps, two switchgear rooms control the electricity, and three travelling cranes service the machinery, one for each side aisle above the pumps and a third for the diesel generators. Two platforms accommodate ventilation equipment for the lower access walkways, and a system of high-level catwalks allows access to all parts and a convenient circuit for visitors. Eleven steel portal frames, founded on the concrete substructure, support the equipment and frame the building volume.

1 *aluminium louvre cladding*
2 *aluminium rainscreen cladding*
3 *aluminium gutter*
4 *aluminium profiled roof cladding*
5 *decorative rail*
6 *diesel air intake terminal*
7 *diesel exhaust flue*
8 *pumpwell ventilation terminal*
9 *steel portal frames*
10 *concrete substructure*
11 *pumpwell ventilation pipe*
12 *travelling crane*
13 *crane access catwalk*
14 *gallery catwalk*
15 *raising mains*
16 *high-level outlet channel*
17 *service access level*
18 *low-level inlet channel*
19 *penstock and retaining barscreen*
20 *submersible pump*

Providing security and protection from the elements, the outer metal skin encloses the single cathedral-like space, 23 metres high, 57 metres long and 29 metres wide. Externally, the roof and walls are conceived as a single surface that can be read as a delicate skin or a monolithic casting. Screens of aluminium louvres and panels express the geometry and rhythm of the structural framing within. The louvres provide a free flow of air that is exhausted at the top of the building through the raised apex.

Section showing concrete substructure with pumps and steel superstructure carrying the generating plant and crane assemblies.

▶ *Structure and lining of the inner face of the external gable.*
▼ *Internal view with crane line.*

The roof is clad in pre-curved aluminium sheeting with a protective zinc coating, while internally a layer of insulation and an inner lining prevent condensation and reduce noise from rain. Eight cylindrical cowls pierce the roof, four on each side, providing ventilation for the diesel generators, while four exhaust flues on one side only contradict the axial symmetry of the building.

The new pumping station is located near its nineteenth-century predecessor designed by Joseph Bazalgette.

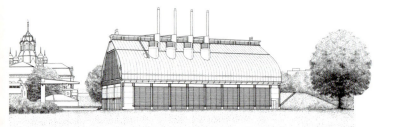

NO 1 PRINCE OF WALES ROAD
London
1995–97

Originally built in 1927 as a technical college, No 1 Prince of Wales Road was adapted and extended by Allies and Morrison for residential use. Photographs in the original college prospectus show a robust interior with large rooms, used as workshops and classrooms, arranged around two discrete internal courtyards and lit by full-height industrial steel windows. By 1995 internal subdivisions and extensions into the courtyards had obscured the qualities of the original structure although the external elevations, though well worn, had remained largely intact.

The project, to provide sixty flats and maisonettes, aimed to restore the clarity of the original building and establish an organisation that was legible, familiar and domestic. The major intervention was the linking of the twin courtyards at ground level by a new entrance lobby leading from the street.

◀ Restored facade to Prince of Wales Road.
▶ View into the central courtyard where a new steel bridge provides access to the flats.

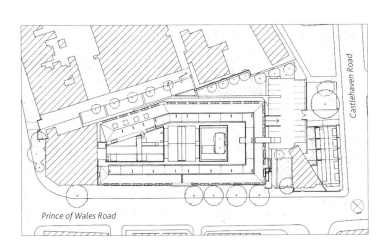

Rather than retaining corridor access to the lower floors, all of the ground- and first-floor flats are now accessed by collegiate-style staircases from the restored courtyards. This allows the flats to face both into the courtyard and out to the street. On the second floor, the original pattern of access from a grand staircase and corridor is preserved. Here maisonettes have been formed by extending upwards into the roof space, and these open onto terraces that overlook the courtyards. The principal living spaces in the apartments extend the full width of the building and, on the second floor, up into the roof structure. Although the apartments vary greatly in layout, each is treated architecturally in a similar manner without trying to disguise the fact that the modern interiors have been inserted into an existing shell, and the detailing of the new construction reinforces this hierarchy.

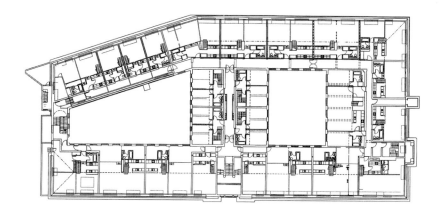

Second floor plan

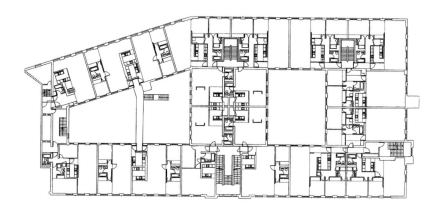

First floor plan

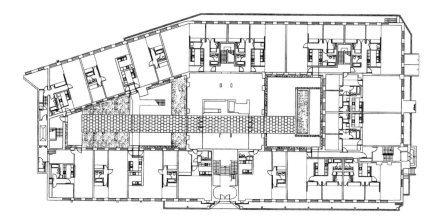

Ground floor plan

▶ View into the larger of the two courtyards where the new stair and bridge provide access to the first-floor flats.
▼ Long section through the courtyards and the central shared reception.

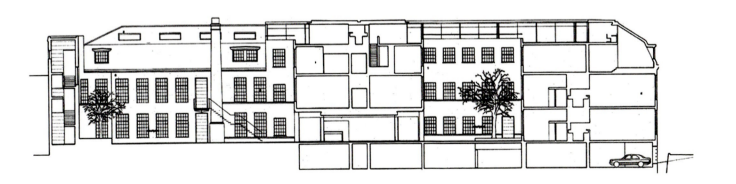

▼ Typical apartment interior with windows to the street and inner courtyard.
▼ Original attic classroom.
▼ First-floor classroom after stripping out the fixtures.

RUTHERFORD INFORMATION SERVICES BUILDING
Goldsmiths College
London
1996–97

The Rutherford Building forms an extension to Goldsmith College's 1980s library on its New Cross campus. The new block provides information technology and language resource facilities to complement the original printed collections. The building integrates with a previously discordant group of post-war buildings – the existing library, the Warmington Tower, and the lozenge-shaped gallery adjacent to the front entrance. In so doing, a small inner courtyard is created to the south of the new building.

In addition to providing much-needed new accommodation, the college was keen to establish a clearer entrance to the library and the campus as well as providing a stronger public identity for the institution as a whole.

◀ *A tall column supports the canopy above and signals the new entrance.*
▶ *View from New Cross Road.*

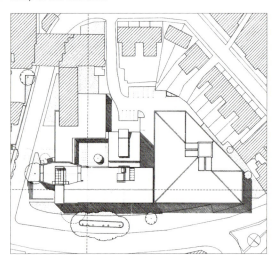

1 entrance
2 administration
3 lecture
4 lending desk
5 existing library
6 courtyard
7 Warmington Tower
8 existing gallery

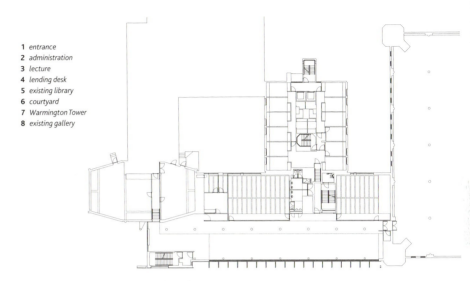

First floor plan

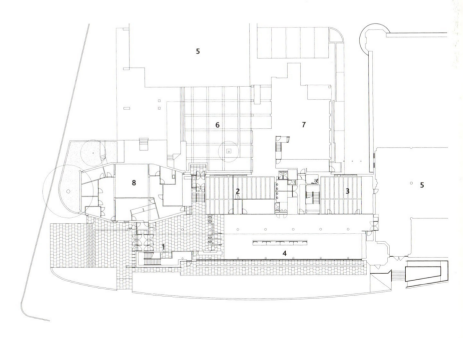

Ground floor plan

Accordingly the three open-plan floors of the building are fully glazed, exposing the intensive computer-based activities to the street. While the north-east orientation of the building eliminates any issues of solar gain, the problem of glare still had to be addressed. External vertical fins made of perforated aluminium, integrated in the two upper floors of the glazed street elevation, allow filtered light deep into the study areas, but preclude direct light from the computer screens. The arrangement of fins nonetheless allows views to the trees that line the street.

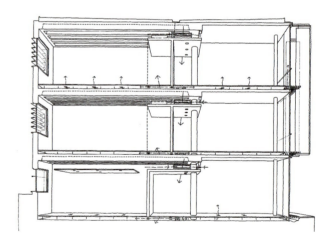

▲ The thermal mass of the concrete structure is exposed so as to mediate temperature fluctuations; the raised floor acts as a plenum for the displacement ventilation system.
◀ Computer desks are aligned perpendicular to the north-facing storey-height glazing to help reduce glare.

◀ Detail showing the junction between the floor and the full-height glazed facade.
▶ External fins by day and night.

The college was keen to avoid reliance on air conditioning for environmental reasons but the levels of pollution and noise from Lewisham Way meant that natural ventilation was not a viable option. Cooling is therefore provided by a displacement ventilation system, with all services distributed within the raised floor plenum. The relatively high thermal mass of the exposed concrete soffit allows heat produced by people and machines during the day to be absorbed, and released slowly at night when temperatures drop, helping to reduce potential peak temperatures and to flatten the overall temperature gradients. Typically on each floor there is an open-plan study area behind the glazed facade, while at the rear there are enclosed teaching spaces and the services and stair core. These spaces have more conventional windows set in a rendered masonry wall. The teaching spaces have a deep ribbed concrete soffit, reflecting the larger structural span and providing a grid for partitioning if they require reconfiguring in the future.

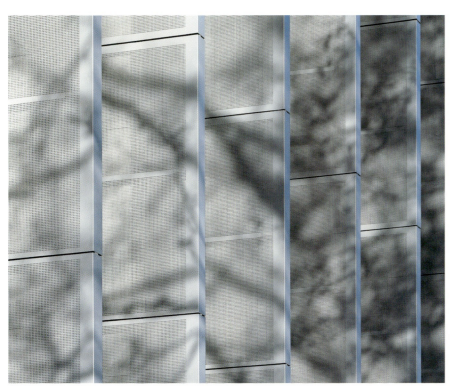

THE PLACE
London
1996–2001

Since 1969 the London School of Contemporary Dance and The Place theatre have been housed on a curious triangular site in a group of interconnected buildings south of Euston Road near Euston Station. The most significant, the Artists' Rifles Drill Hall, was designed by RW Edis in 1889.

While the ad hoc nature of the buildings lent the school a certain informal charm, the quality of the dance studios was severely compromised by the configuration of the spaces, while the public face and foyer of the theatre were deemed insufficiently welcoming.

This project sought to address these problems with the insertion of a new structure with six generous studios on the north-east corner of the site and by reconfiguring the reception spaces to the Drill Hall to create a more effective public entrance. Two new lifts also allowed full disabled access to the building for the first time.

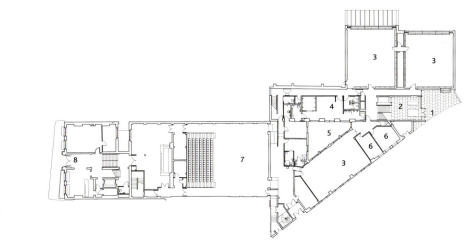

1 school entrance
2 reception
3 studio
4 changing rooms
5 lightwell
6 office
7 auditorium
8 auditorium entrance

▲ Interior of dance studio.
▼ Section through existing building and new entrance and studio building.

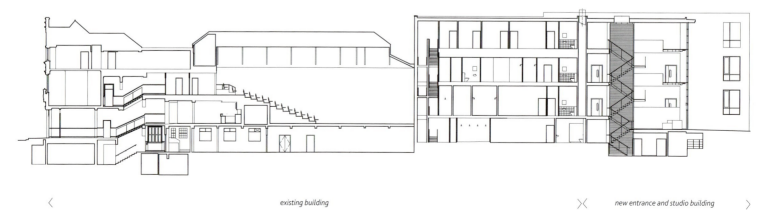

existing building   new entrance and studio building

More significantly however the project created a new focus for the life of the school in the form of the triple-height entrance space on Flaxman Terrace. The space is overlooked by the balconies that give access to the three floors of studios, by the open staircase that links to the remainder of the school's facilities and by 'stretching zones', wide landings where students can exercise during the intervals between classes, that are clearly visible through the glass wall of the entrance facade.

The studios are simple spaces with glass block walls to the north that allow filtered daylight but protect privacy (the windows of an adjacent hotel are just metres away). Low-velocity mechanical ventilation is provided through a central duct while opening windows allow students and staff to enjoy the outside air between classes.

▶ *Triple-height space with stretching zone landings overlooking the street.*
▼ *Section through studios and entrance space.*

TATE BRITAIN LANDSCAPE
London
1997–2001

The new entrance to Tate Britain, on its south flank facing Atterbury Street, provides direct access to the lower-level exhibition spaces within the north-west quadrant of the gallery building.

The entrance is reached by a six-metre-wide incision in the ground, parallel to the facade, comprising on one side a wide stone staircase and on the other a ramp. A continuous ribbon of glass, translucent below ground level and transparent above, marks the fissure.

The new entrance forms part of a wider project to enhance the public use of the gardens that surround the gallery. On the main Millbank frontage an adjustment in the alignment of the railings has allowed a more generous space at the base of the main flight of steps and also a more fluid connection with the

◀ *New entrance stair and ramp*
▼ *Section model showing the glass wall to the ramp and stair which also forms the balustrade along Atterbury Street.*

◄ By day, the glass wall appears transparent above ground and opaque below.
▲ By night, the back-lit glass wall illuminates the stair and ramp.

gardens to each side. This arrangement emphasises the presence of both the Atterbury Street and the Clore Gallery entrances and provides for the first time level access for visitors in wheelchairs to the gardens. The orthogonal geometry of the new landscape grows out of the alignments of the existing buildings and the detailing of the surfaces, like that of the Atterbury Street entrance, is conceived as a series of incisions into the horizontal datum of the ground. Extending on each side of the main entrance are two wide flower beds which provide a changing visual focus for the gardens. The planting, which changes with each season, was designed by landscape architect Brita von Schoenaich.

CENTENARY BUILDING HORNIMAN MUSEUM
London
1997–2002

Over the course of the last century the Horniman Museum developed in an ad hoc way with facilities added as needs became apparent and funds became available. While there were many gains in this process, there were also losses. The clarity and integrity of the original buildings were inevitably compromised and none of the new additions matched the quality of their illustrious predecessors. On a more practical level the new spaces were often inadequate while the changes in floor levels between old and new created endless access difficulties for the public and curatorial staff alike.

The injection of funds made possible by the National Lottery, together with money raised by other friends and supporters, gave the opportunity to review this process and to replace the various additions with a single new extension more closely tailored to the museum's needs. More generous in both scale and aspiration than the accommodation it replaced, the Centenary Building was accordingly aligned with Charles Harrison Townsend's remarkable original buildings. The new extension not only provided some entirely new facilities – including a new temporary exhibitions gallery – but it also replaced, with greatly improved facilities, a number of other functions. These include a new, much enlarged gallery for the musical instrument collection, a new shop and cafe and a new education department immediately adjacent to the new handling collection, itself located in the original library in the upper level of the Emslie Horniman Hall. In addition a new lift connects all the existing and new floors, making the entire museum accessible to all visitors.

But perhaps the most significant consequence of the new extension was the reorientation of the museum towards the gardens to the west, allowing for the first time a direct relationship between them, something Frederick Horniman had envisaged a century before.

The entrance on the west side of the new extension, approached through the gardens, establishes a new cross-axis within the museum which links with the original staircase that connects the South Hall and North Hall. This route is reinforced by the location of the cafe, which can be separately accessed from the gardens, and by a large window formed within the museum that provides a view out towards the nineteenth-century conservatory. It also links with a new double-height space at the heart of the museum which connects the new and old parts.

The new building extends the sequence of linear galleries and public spaces and establishes a new relationship with the gardens.

1 original museum
2 1912 extension
3 new building
4 temporary building
5 Michael Horniman conservation centre

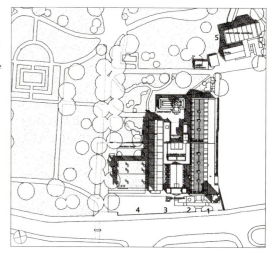

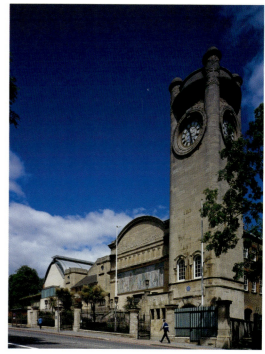

The new building presents a third stone gable to the street frontage.

▲ Cafe interior.
▶ The new entrance from the gardens is set within a cloistered threshold that also provides separate access to the cafe, exhibition space and education centre.

Many of the new gallery spaces in the extension are located below ground level and designed to receive a minimum of daylight – the aim is to control light levels to protect the sensitive objects on display. But in the other public spaces natural light is introduced wherever possible, creating an open and welcoming atmosphere.

Externally, the extension is constructed using a similar palette of materials to that Townsend employed in the original buildings – Doulting Stone for the street facade, red brick for the side elevations (just as Townsend used yellow London stocks for the less significant walls), and metal for the curved roofs of the North and South Halls. The new extension also has a vaulted roof, in this case with daylight introduced at the apex, a configuration that is legible in the London Road elevation where the roof seems to float above the masonry below.

The new entrance elevation to the gardens comprises a series of openings in the brickwork elevation, each responding to the particular function within. In the centre of the elevation a deep recess identifies the public entrance and provides a route to a separate entrance to the education centre. Just as the design of the new building has evolved in response to the gardens, the new landscape that surrounds the building has been reshaped to link the two key elements of Horniman's bequest together.

▶ Main entrance and bookshop window; the repetitive rhythm of the masonry wall is broken to create a wider bay which marks the entrance.
▼ The scale of the gable facing the street is tempered by the projecting bay, which lets light into the gallery and forms the setting for a seat overlooking the entrance garden.

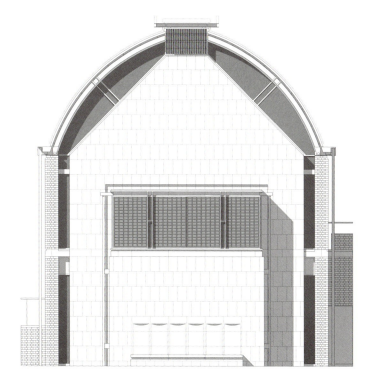

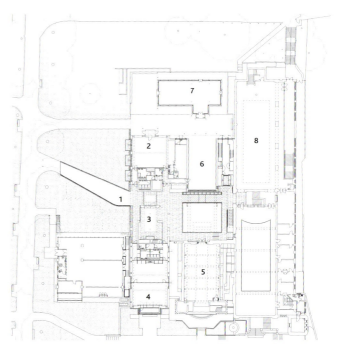

Ground floor plan

1 *main entrance*
2 *cafe*
3 *shop*
4 *education centre*
5 *hands-on base*
6 *conservatory terrace*
7 *conservatory*
8 *galleries*

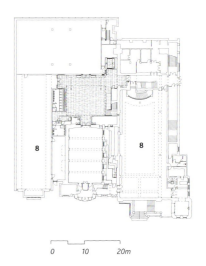

Basement plan

◀ View from the central orientation space, across the ramp and into courtyard, with the conservatory beyond.
◀ View of entrance cloister from the shop.
▶ Windows to the cafe incorporate louvred panels to each side, with inner shutters to facilitate night-time cooling.

Tall windows on the north elevation give generous light levels in the conservation laboratory and design studio.

MICHAEL HORNIMAN BUILDING
HORNIMAN MUSEUM

London
1997–2002

Construction of the Michael Horniman Building formed the first phase of the extensive works at the south London museum. It was built on a discrete site within the museum gardens prior to the commencement of the main works.

The simple form and materials of the building reflect both the nature of the site, deep within the landscape of the gardens, and the utility of its purpose. This is an everyday, working building with no public function, and this is expressed in the simplicity of the detailing – for instance, the metal south-facing monopitch roof, which brings north light deep into the plan on the upper floors, remains unarticulated and flush with the vertical western red cedar cladding.

The ground floor entrance lobby connects a loading bay and entrance to the north with a staff entrance that is accessed from an existing upper level terrace to the south. The central stair, which provides access to all levels of the building, subdivides and organises the plan into its respective functions: a layout space and workshop on the ground floor and the laboratory and exhibition studio on the first floor.

Section

1 workshop
2 staff entrance
3 layout space
4 laboratory
5 exhibition studio
6 loading bay

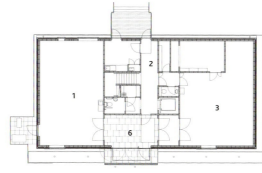

Ground floor plan

First floor plan

SOUTH HILL PARK ARTS CENTRE
Bracknell
1997–2001

South Hill Park, an eighteenth-century country house in Berkshire, was extensively remodelled in the late nineteenth century and became an arts centre in the 1960s. Allies and Morrison's more radical restructuring provided an opportunity to explore more fully the potential of the original building.

The key intervention, at the heart of the building where a dark lightwell previously allowed minimal daylight into the centre of the plan, is the creation of a new atrium space, providing a venue for events. At ground level the atrium connects to the cafe and bar that open out to a terrace and gardens through a new glazed screen inserted within a row of existing Tuscan columns. At first-floor level the atrium is overlooked by a gallery that provides access to the various studio spaces and makes explicit the diversity of activities taking place within the arts centre.

Beyond the atrium, a new pottery and printmaking workshop have been created within the walled enclosure of

A glass clerestory window to the pottery and print-making workshop rises above the retained walls of the original kitchen garden.

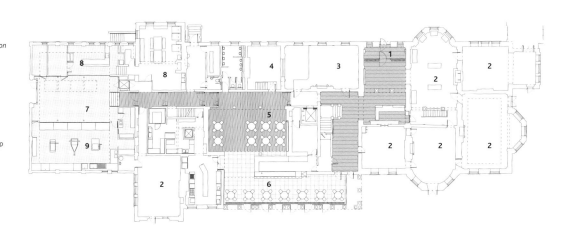

1 entrance and reception
2 gallery spaces and function rooms
3 cinema
4 projection room
5 new atrium
6 cafe and bar
7 kitchen courtyard
8 pottery workshop
9 printmaking workshop

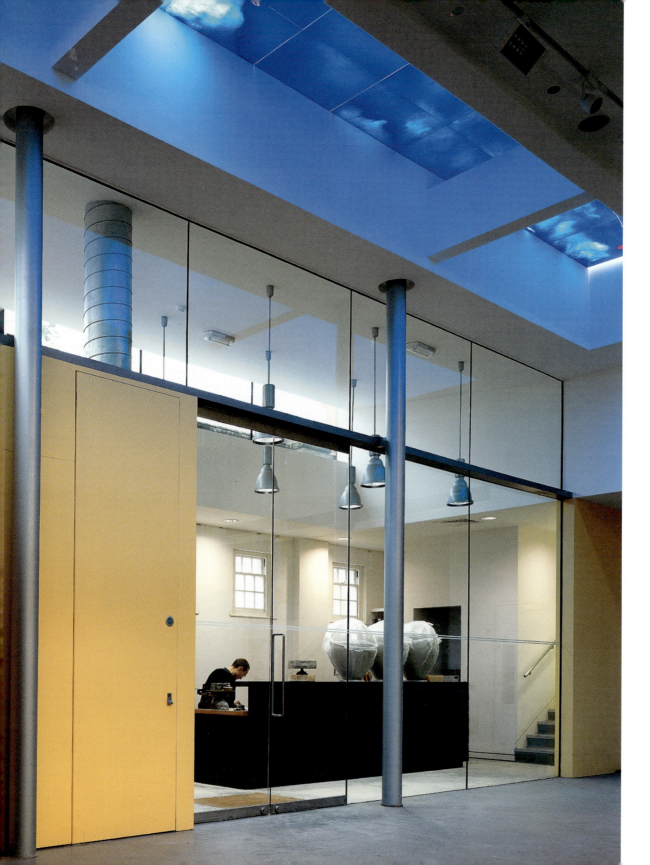

the original kitchen courtyard. A simple flat roof, supported on steel columns, floats above the original masonry and clerestory glazing, allowing light into the interior and capturing views of the surrounding trees. Full-height glazed screens separate the individual spaces and establish a sequence of workmanlike rooms. Within the old kitchen courtyard, a rooflight illuminates an installation by glass artist Martin Donlin.

▲ Print-making workshop.
▲ The cafe/bar opens onto the gardens through a glazed screen that corresponds to the bays of the existing loggia.
▶ The new atrium space has been formed within a former external light court.
◀ Full-height glazed walls open the pottery workshop to view.

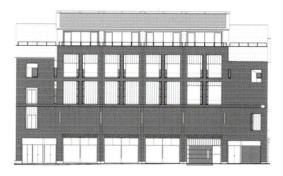

◄ The scale and rhythm of the new facade responds to its Victorian neighbours.
▲ New side elevation.
▲ A new entrance has been inserted into the retained facade.

THE HOSPITAL
London
1997–2003

Microsoft co-founder Paul Allen and British musician Dave Stewart conceived the idea for a single building with all the facilities that would enable creative artists to work efficiently and comfortably. They sought a location in central London, midway between the fashionable warehouses of the East End and the film studios of Elstree and Shepperton to the west of the city. They found a run-down building near Covent Garden, a maternity hospital for London's poor that had later become a teaching hospital, but which had remained unused since 1992, ruined and filled with the echoes of its past.

The facades facing Endell Street and the long return on Shorts Gardens to the north were retained in the redevelopment, whereas a substantial frontage of three buildings on Betterton Street, the next road to the south, was demolished and replaced.

The required facilities included a sound stage for live recording and broadcast, large enough for a full orchestra playing a soundtrack to a film projected in the same space or a live television broadcast of a recording artist and audience, a separate recording studio, a luxurious screening room, a private members' club, a restaurant and bar, overnight apartments for artists working in the building, state-of-the-art editing suites, an art gallery and offices.

The double-height reception, within which the rear face of the retained corner is exposed, provides a lofty and dramatic entrance to the otherwise dense plan. Two lifts and a cantilevered steel staircase link this space with the upper floors. Lift landings open onto a balcony that connects the accommodation back to the entrance space via a narrow top-lit atrium. Each floor is divided into three parts, with substantial rooms to the north and south flanks and cores within the central third. The main sound stage occupies much of the double basement space with circulation, support rooms and control rooms arranged around the outside.

The double-height entrance space has been formed behind the retained facade.

The masterplan defined a narrow lane that aligns with the north transept of St Paul's Cathedral; the brick facade of St Martin's Court is on the east side.

ST MARTIN'S COURT PATERNOSTER SQUARE

London
1996–2003

In 1940 Luftwaffe bombing caused a devastating fire that razed a substantial district north of St Paul's Cathedral. In the 1960s the area was eventually redeveloped with a characteristic series of office buildings designed by William Holford but, by the 1990s, these had become outmoded and unloved. As part of William Whitfield's masterplan for the complete redevelopment of Paternoster Square, Allies and Morrison was commissioned to design a building at number 10 Paternoster Row.

The design intention was to avoid the monumental and develop a series of facades that, while satisfying the internal planning discipline of the building, derive from the context so that the public realm is given an equivalent significance to the content of the building.

The building has retail units on the ground and lower ground levels, and six floors of offices above, all planned around an atrium with a foyer at its base. Within the roof-lit atrium is a

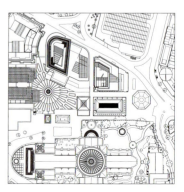

balconied elevator wall, faced in European oak panels. The balconies look down over the atrium floor, paved in fossil-bed Derbyshire limestone, and up to a series of terraces. These terraces, a necessary response to the stringent rules governing St Paul's heights, afford spectacular views of the dome of the cathedral.

The entrances to the offices are from Newgate Street and Paternoster Row and the remaining perimeter is given over to shops and cafes. The primary facades on Newgate Street and Cheapside are clad in Portland stone and the two minor facades to Paternoster Row and Queens Head Passage are built in brick. Here, consistent with the masterplan's intention to recreate something of the long-gone medieval character, two new lanes are formed. The first, 7.5 metres wide, runs east to west from St Paul's underground station to the new Paternoster Square. The second, running north-south and only 6 metres wide, aligns with the north transept of St Paul's, framing a significant view of the cathedral.

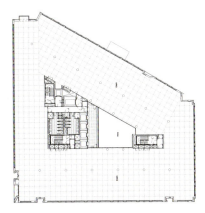

Second floor plan

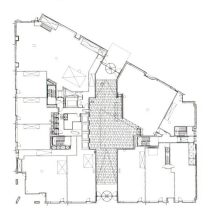

Ground floor plan
Two entrances are set between perimeter shops that are serviced from a shared yard at basement level.

HOLDEN HOUSE
London
1997–2000

Occupying a prominent corner site at the junction of Oxford Street and Rathbone Place, this listed building provides five floors of office space over the street level retail space. Designed by Charles Holden and Percy Adams in 1910, the building was originally planned with front doors for both uses facing Oxford Street, but serviced through large gates on Rathbone Place.

Over the years Oxford Street has become increasingly dedicated to retail uses with busy pedestrian traffic, and the appropriateness of the address for office use came into question. A major consideration in Allies and Morrison's refurbishment was therefore the relocation of the office entrance to the quieter Rathbone Place. The consequential shift in the centre of gravity of the plan allowed easy and generous access through the original carriageway to an interior lightwell. This open yard was roofed and glazed to form an office foyer and new lifts and a stair were inserted. This in turn released more useable space for both the shops on the ground floor and the offices above.

The original gates on Rathbone Place were restored and a bridge now provides a long threshold to the foyer. New lifts are enclosed by deep timber slats lit within the shaft. Above this new double-height entrance hall the lifts rise in a glass shaft to further bridges serving the office floors. Here the services are located beneath a new raised floor to maximise the available headroom and allowing the original ceiling beams to be left exposed.

▲ Section model showing entrance sequence from the street to the foyer, a new space containing the new lifts within the original lightwell.
◄ The louvred timber lift enclosure is visible from the street entrance.

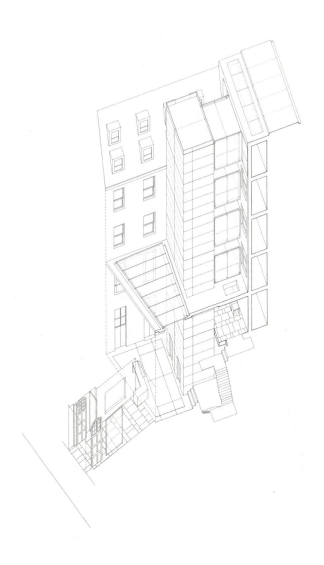

▲ Axonometric showing route from street, entrance hall, lift shaft and lightwell.
▶ Detail of lift enclosure.

BLACKBURN HOUSE
London
1997–99

The clients' brief was to convert their early Victorian west London house to provide a backdrop for their art collection. The existing spaces in the house were disjointed and insular and the entrance and staircase lacked the generosity evident elsewhere.

New linings were inserted into the Victorian shell to re-shape the spaces and create new connections. This strategy of distinguishing between new and old provides a language of layers that sets up a dialogue with the surviving features of the house, and helps achieve an appropriate level of richness that complements the character of the original.

A cantilevered precast concrete stair has been inserted into the enlarged hall, creating a shaft of light through the house that incorporates the landings and relates to the garden within a single vertical space.

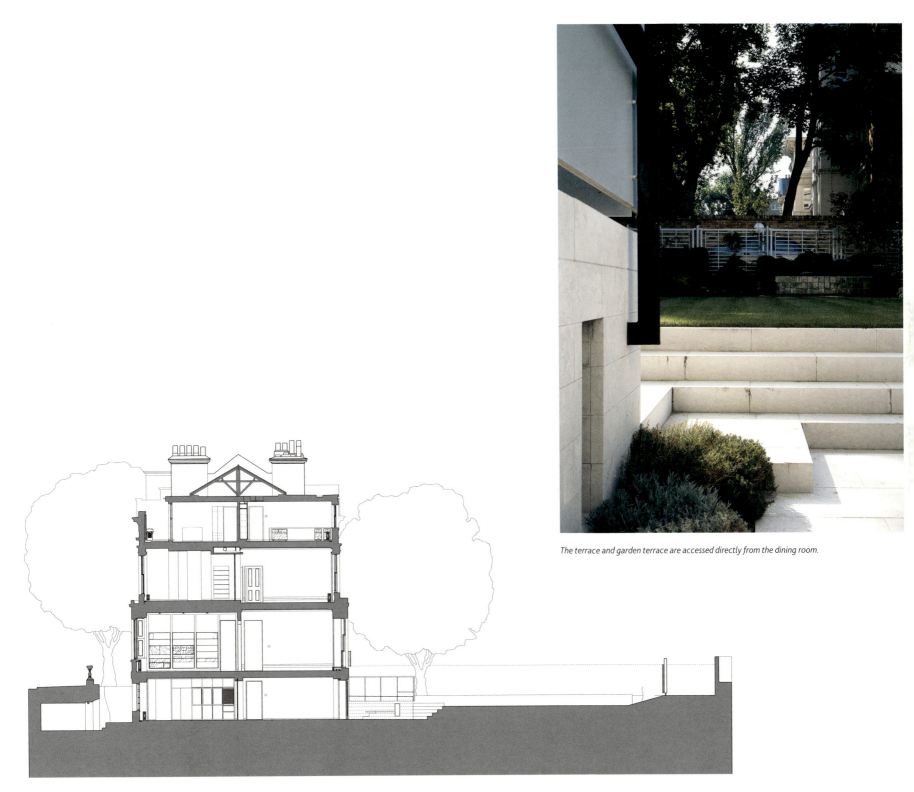

The terrace and garden terrace are accessed directly from the dining room.

1 dining room
2 kitchen
3 laundry
4 store
5 hall
6 study
7 drawing room
8 master bedroom
9 bathroom
10 dressing room

First floor plan

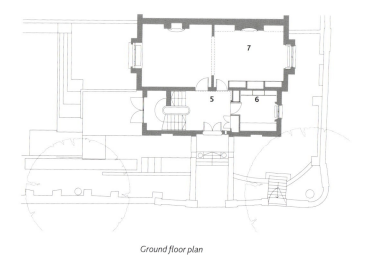

Ground floor plan

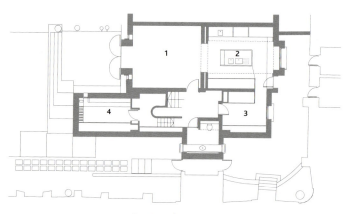

Basement plan

Cantilevered concrete stair with plastered soffits and thin metal balustrade. The plaster of the surrounding walls is set back to receive the profile of the stair treads.

BLACKWELL
Windermere
1998–2001

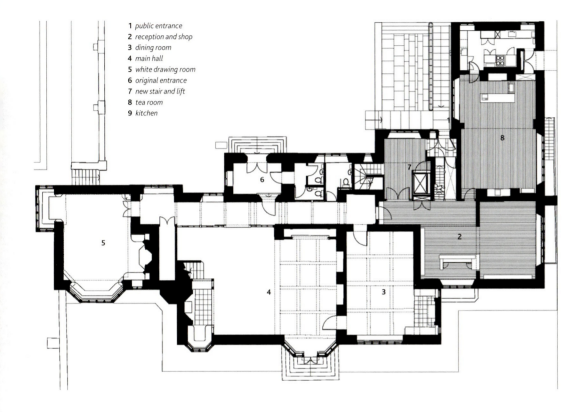

1 public entrance
2 reception and shop
3 dining room
4 main hall
5 white drawing room
6 original entrance
7 new stair and lift
8 tea room
9 kitchen

Designed by MH Baillie Scott in 1898-1900, Blackwell is one of the most important surviving houses of the Arts and Crafts period. In 1999 its owner, the Lakeland Trust, commissioned Allies and Morrison to restore the listed house and adapt it for use as a gallery for the applied arts.

The significance of Blackwell lies in its realisation of Baillie Scott's notion of an 'artistic house' and, in the restoration, the priority was to recover the 'soul of the house' and its 'atmosphere of deep-seated calm' at the same time as revealing the wealth of original detail in the interior spaces. Rich colours have been exposed and metalwork, stained glass, timber panelling and printed wall coverings restored.

The more modest service rooms were converted to provide new visitor facilities. The tea room has been located in the original kitchens, the butler's pantries provide

reception and sales areas, the laundry became the public toilet facilities. New elements such as the internal fire escape stair have been treated as modern insertions.

In terms of the landscape, Baillie Scott had transformed a rocky hillside into a garden by employing a series of concentric terraces. The new scheme adds to these layers with the creation of a new entrance courtyard and a sunken parking area. The replanting scheme includes the same species of local wild flowers and trees that had featured in Baillie Scott's original interior decorative scheme.

▲ The restored interior of the White Drawing Room with window seat overlooking Lake Windermere.
◄ East-west section through the main public rooms.

▲ A new staircase provides access to office space created in the attic rooms.
◀ Baillie Scott planned the house as a sequence of spaces.

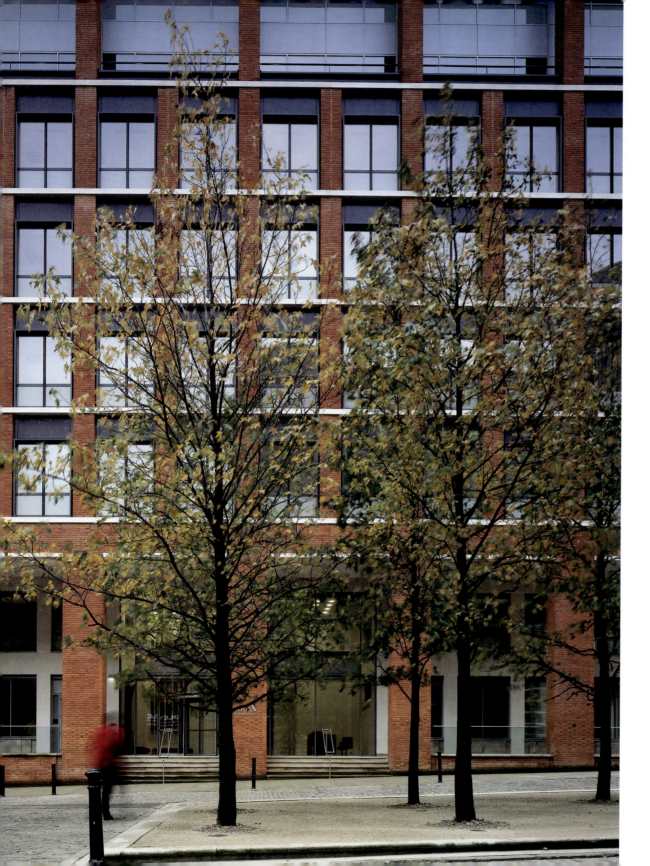

6 BRINDLEYPLACE
Birmingham
1997–2000

Occupying a key site within this pioneering urban regeneration project, 6 Brindleyplace comprises eight floors of offices set above two car parking floors. The building faces both of the principal public spaces of Brindleyplace and Oozells Square and, although planned symmetrically, the base of the building addresses these two spaces differently. On the south side the ground floor is occupied by restaurants opening out onto Oozells Square, while on the north side the main entrance leads off a colonnade, continuous within two adjacent buildings, which aligns Brindleyplace itself. From the entrance, a main stair leads to the floor of the five-storey roof-lit atrium. Timber balustrades on three sides act as balconies overlooking the space and a timber bridge on the fourth links the two sides of the atrium with the core and the lifts.

Compositionally, the facades reflect both the cross-sectional interior organisation and the nature of the exterior spaces they address. Each of the four facades conforms to a tripartite order in which the colonnaded base supports the four office floors of the atrium and a recessed two-storey 'attic' represents the upper external courtyard. The elevations facing the two squares are composed entirely of brick piers and storey-height glazing separated by string courses. This open 'frame-like' character appropriate to the public space is distinct from the elevations facing the two side lanes. Here the addition of a brick balustrade and consequential reduction in glazing suggest a more 'wall-like' and subordinate character.

◄ Facade to Brindleyplace.
► Atrium space and reception.

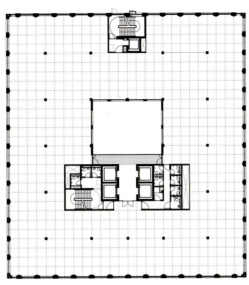
Typical upper floor plan

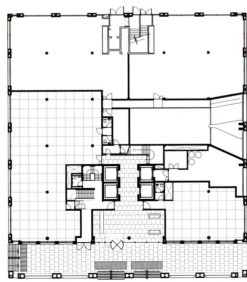
Ground floor plan

169

SCOTCH MALT WHISKY SOCIETY
London
1999–2000

A series of rooms set on the upper floors of a Victorian artisan building in Farringdon provides the setting for a significant Scottish event: the convivial, serious but straightforward task of tasting malt whisky. This is neither a bar nor a club and it is devoid of brands. Two rows of numbered, but otherwise identically labelled, bottles carefully set out behind a bar are the only indication of the function of the space and the purpose of the society.

From the street, a simple horizontally-boarded timber door with a stainless steel rod handle is set into a double-height glass screen, giving access to the stair linking the three levels of the building. A limestone floor folds into a short flight to a solid half-landing from which a series of simple oak treads on steel pegs lead to the principal floor. The bar, occupying one side of the main room, is made of limestone fronted with vertical timber boards and protected by a stainless steel kick rail. Original details such as the window shutters have been restored, lighting is discreet, and the furniture is unostentatiously domestic and comfortable. A small private nook with bench seating is linked to the end of the bar. Upstairs, space is provided for courses and private functions together with a small office and kitchen.

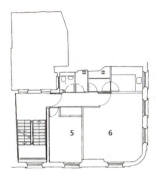

Second floor plan

First floor plan

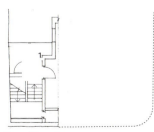

Ground floor plan

1 *entrance*
2 *lobby*
3 *bar*
4 *members room*
5 *office*
6 *private room*

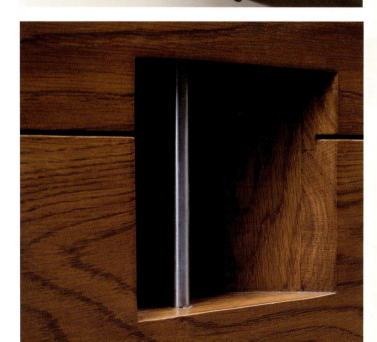

▶ *Detail of new stair and front door handle.*

COWDRAY PARK GOLF CLUB
West Sussex
1999–2001

Cowdray Park is set within an Area of Outstanding Natural Beauty on the West Sussex Downs. The proposed new golf clubhouse is to be sited at the edge of the relocated eighteenth green, where the land slopes steeply away from the level of the course.

The entrance, changing rooms, games room, and other ancillary functions are located at the lower level with direct access from the car park. The upper level opens out onto the first tee and the eighteenth green. Here the lounge, dining room, bar and professionals' shop are planned as a sequence of interconnecting rooms. Organised around a central kitchen and bar, they are tightly planned to maximise efficiency and minimise running costs. The walls to the public spaces at this level are largely glazed, with doors opening onto the terrace. There are fine views across the course and south towards the ruins of Cowdray House.

The roof consists of a single all-encompassing monopitch, supported on steel columns. This large plane is broken only by the suite of administrative offices that rise above the body of the main building at first-floor level. Again, a continuous balcony overlooks the course. The building is serviced from the rear where a small service yard at the lower level gives access to a series of stores. From here a hoist and stair provides a direct connection to the kitchen and bar.

The 12-room Dormy House is designed as a discrete building, but close to the clubhouse. Sited adjacent to the car park for easy access for visitors and with a view over the driving range, the Dormy House is planned on two levels with bedroom suites served by a single-loaded corridor. Architecturally, it is treated as a relatively modest structure, subservient in height, form and material to the clubhouse.

The simple monopitch roof, which floats above the club room, is pierced by the volume of the offices and terrace.

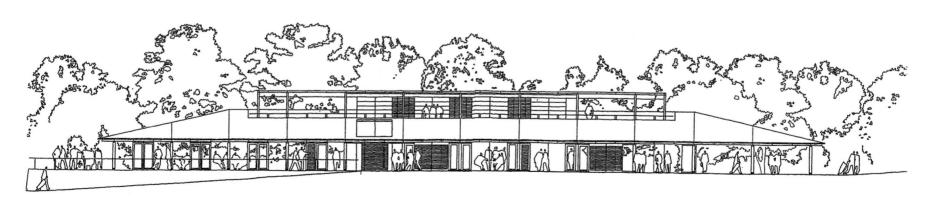

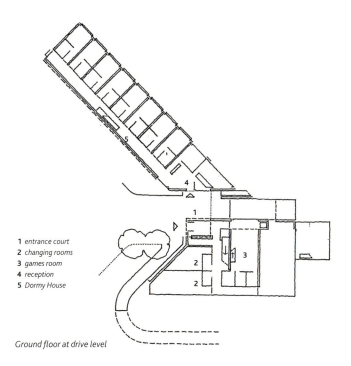

1 entrance court
2 changing rooms
3 games room
4 reception
5 Dormy House

Ground floor at drive level

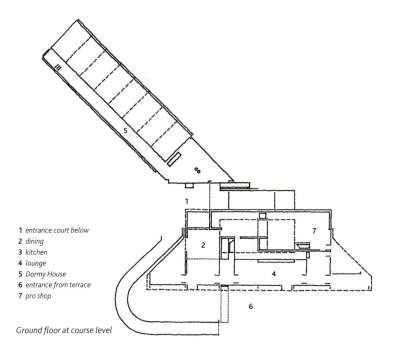

1 entrance court below
2 dining
3 kitchen
4 lounge
5 Dormy House
6 entrance from terrace
7 pro shop

Ground floor at course level

FULHAM BROADWAY
London
1999–2002

Architecturally, the facade provides the interface where the discipline of the internal organisation of a building reaches a resolution with the outside world, making a response to its context. Located on the busy Fulham Broadway and opposite the muscular stone frontage of the Old Town Hall, this new intervention fronts a shopping centre whose mall leads directly to the entrance of the underground station. The facade therefore has a triple role: to form one side of a significant street, to reveal the shopping centre and to represent the station entrance.

The four-storey facade, three storeys of which are visible from the street, consists of eight seven-metre bays split asymmetrically (5:3) by a three-storey glazed entrance to the mall. While the transparency of this entrance represents the interior world of the shopping mall, the stone facade of the eight bays, with the

◀ *Facade model showing typical bay and entrance to the underground station.*
▶ *Retail frontage to Fulham Broadway.*

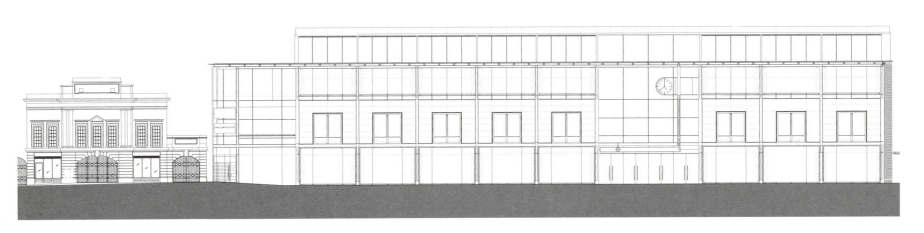

addition of a large clock at high level over the entrance, suggests a more civic purpose and signals the entrance to the station.

The tripartite composition comprises a glazed ground floor (with signage set behind the shop fronts), a first floor of stack-bonded limestone panels with bay windows that project over the pavement, and a recessed attic storey beneath a projecting metal canopy that runs the full length of the elevation. Details such as the lined openings to the ground floor, the handrail assemblies to the second-floor balcony, and the clock are made from anodised aluminium.

◀ *Elevation to Fulham Broadway with underground station.*
▶ *Facade study and station entrance detail.*

MILTON KEYNES COLLEGE
Buckinghamshire
1999–2002

Milton Keynes College's new Bletchley campus is located on the site of a number of dilapidated 1960s buildings. The plan of the new college comprises three distinct external spaces: an entrance forecourt marked by a colonnade; a central courtyard aligned on three sides by the main building and on the front by a swathe of mature woodland; and a less formal yard containing a separate workshop building.

The central courtyard provides the focus of the new college. On its east side a triple-height cloister defines a principal circulation route from where a sequence of staircases rise to the upper-floor teaching spaces. The wall to the cloister is fully glazed and an internal timber brise-soleil modulates the light within the space. In winter, solar gain passing through the single-glazed wall contributes to the heating of the interior; in summer, opening vents at the top of the space allow convection currents to draw excess heat out. This strategy is key to the satisfactory operation of the 12-metre-deep teaching spaces, providing natural ventilation both at the external window-wall and via the atrium to the south.

The external wall treatment varies according to context, creating diversity without complexity on a comparatively low budget. The outermost facades are clad in lapped grey fibre-cement panels. Elevations facing the courtyards, in contrast, are detailed in European larch.

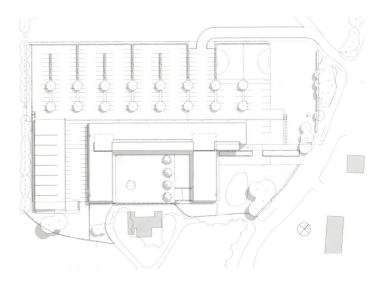

The triple-height colonnade forms an extended entrance to the college.

◀ Detail of facade to classrooms and single-glazed elevation to the cloister.
▼ Perspective view of the entrance courtyard.

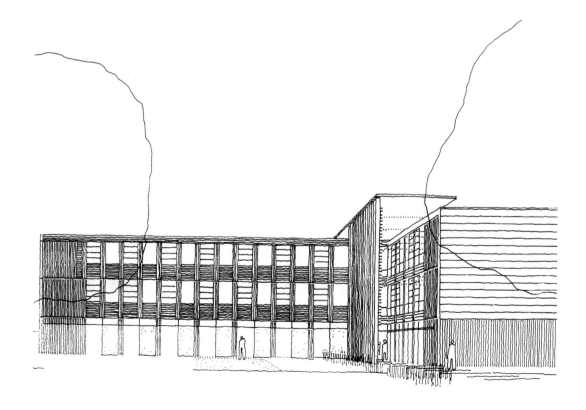

The principal circulation space or 'cloister' is an unheated space, providing an intermediate buffer between the changing external environment and the controlled conditions of the teaching spaces. The fully glazed wall incorporates an internal timber screen that helps prevent overheating in summer.

NEWNHAM COLLEGE LIBRARY
Cambridge
1999

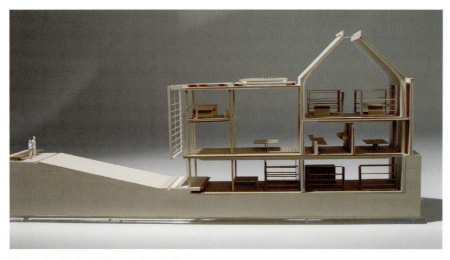

Cross section showing the library, facing onto the sunken courtyard, with reading rooms to the right.

This competition project was concerned with the intricate interconnection of three existing buildings – the original Newnham College library, with its glass-floored reading galleries, a U-shaped residential court of late-nineteenth-century college buildings, both designed by Basil Champneys, and the Rare Books Library, completed in 1983 by van Heyningen and Haward.

While the body of the proposed new library – with its two-storey brick structure and pitched metal roof – was conceived as an eastern extension to the original Yates Thompson building, the main entrance was oriented south towards the existing courtyard, where its facade would provide a new focus. Accordingly, the identity of the library within the overall configuration of the college would be enhanced.

The entrance incorporates a double-height space, overlooked by the main library desk and containing functions such as the catalogue, an area for exhibitions and display, and lockers for visiting scholars. From here access can be gained to the original library and, via a new staircase, to the main book stacks and reader spaces on the first floor. A variety of reader spaces was provided, ranging from a room for computer-based study to more intimate carrels located above the library corridor with views across the courtyard.

The basement level library faces out onto a sunken garden carved out of the courtyard space. A gentle landscaped bank leads up from the building to the new perimeter footpath that encircles the space.

The courtyard elevation is seen as a counterpoint to the red brickwork of the other three sides, a white figure on a red ground, a motif employed extensively by Champneys elsewhere within the college buildings. The elevation is characterised by a filigree screen of metalwork that shades and protects the glazed wall behind.

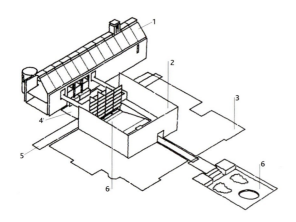

1 library extension
2 courtyard
3 Sidgwick Hall
4 entrance hall
5 library corridor
6 sunken garden

The new library completes the fourth side of an existing courtyard, within which the landscape is excavated to allow light into the basement level.

THE NEWSROOM
GUARDIAN AND OBSERVER ARCHIVE
London
1999–2002

The new glazed entrance screen is set behind full-height openings in the retained facade.

Located in Clerkenwell, the Newsroom housed the archives of the Guardian and Observer newspapers, together with an education and visitor centre, until their move to King's Cross in 2008.

The public facility is contained within the shell of a nineteenth-century warehouse in which a central courtyard had been reclaimed to provide top-lit internal space for temporary exhibitions.
To either side is a lecture space and the environmentally controlled archive space.

The new street entrance is set back behind the brick piers of the original facade, forming a colonnade that expresses the accessible nature of the building. A cafe is located adjacent to the entrance.

At the back of the site a new garden was inserted, tightly framed by party walls to the adjacent buildings. This provides a source of daylight to the education and administrative areas while also drawing the visitor into the interior. The route to the education and administrative areas is framed by glass cabinets which containi bound copies of the Guardian dating back to its founding in 1821.

1 *colonnade*
2 *entrance/foyer*
3 *administration*
4 *classrooms*
5 *main exhibition space*
6 *courtyard*

◀ *Glass cabinets contain bound archive copies of the Guardian newspaper.*

▼ *The steel and glass facade to the rear courtyard provides light and ventilation to the deep interior.*

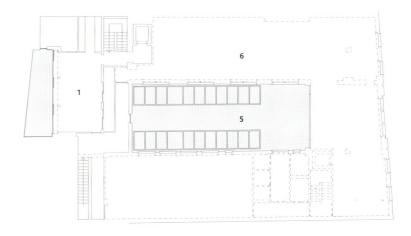

First floor plan

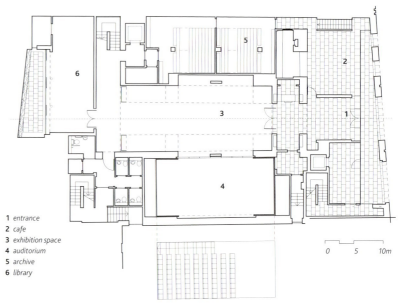

1 *entrance*
2 *cafe*
3 *exhibition space*
4 *auditorium*
5 *archive*
6 *library*

Ground floor plan

ONE PICCADILLY GARDENS
Manchester
1999–2003

Piccadilly Gardens forms a significant component in the regeneration of Manchester's public realm. The new landscaped square is framed on its north side by a seven-storey office building that also protects it from the busy thoroughfare of Portland Street. The entire ground level facing the square is animated by restaurants, bars and shops, and a diagonal public route bisects the building and leads to the office entrance foyers. From here a stair leads to the first floor where the office space is planned around an atrium. The building is capable of single occupation or subdivision into floors or part-floors.

The facades are composed in two parts: an inner layer of glass and metal, reflecting the potential internal subdivision, and a more substantial outer layer of red brick, enclosing the structure. While the two layers both fold within their thickness, the inner layer further distorts to announce and accommodate the diagonal route. The outer layer has a tripartite composition with double-height base and attic storeys.

The different contexts of the north and south facades are also acknowledged in the composition. The open frame-like facade to Piccadilly Gardens contrasts with the wall-like facade to Portland Street in which the outer face of each bay folds back from the column to an inner layer. The dimensional rhythm of both layers contains an inherent asymmetry which, when overlaid, inflects towards the diagonal route through the building.

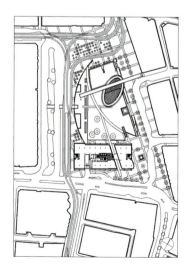

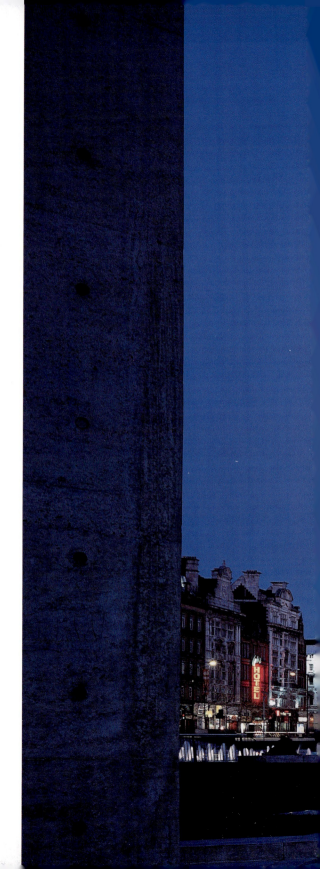

◄ The south facade provides a robust edge to the street.
▼ Detail of ground floor colonnade.

1 offices
2 restaurant
3 reception
4 restaurant/retail use
5 plant

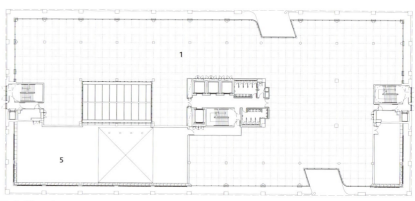

Typical floor plan

Ground floor plan

The atrium and main staircase are located within the heart of the building.

LONDON COLLEGE OF COMMUNICATION
Elephant & Castle, London
1998–2003

Roof plan

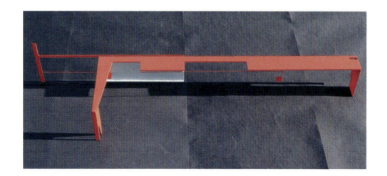

Following a limited competition Allies and Morrison were appointed to develop a masterplan for the consolidation and regeneration of the Elephant & Castle campus of the London College of Printing (now the London College of Communication).

The first phase of the project involved two discrete components. The new teaching block allowed the relocation of media facilities from Clerkenwell to the Elephant & Castle campus, consolidating the entire college onto one site, while the new 'street', which includes a new main entrance, ties together all of the existing college buildings while providing a central focus for the campus as a whole.

The second phase involved the extensive modification and fit-out of the new and existing spaces to meet the college's immediate academic needs, including the provision of a number of specialised facilities. To accommodate the ever-changing requirements related to the delivery of higher education, the new facilities have been designed to allow for maximum flexibility of use.

◀ *Model of the steel armature that marks the new entrance and the start of the 'street'.*
▶ *The new triple-height entrance is inserted between the existing campus buildings.*

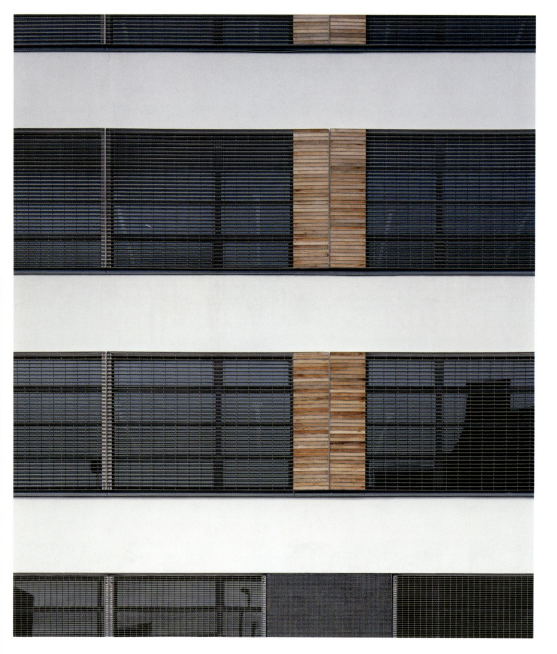

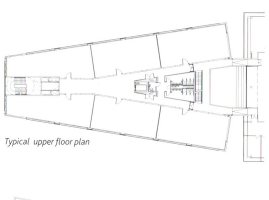
Typical upper floor plan

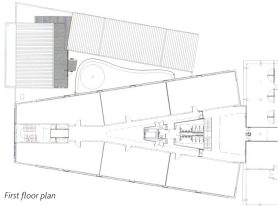
First floor plan

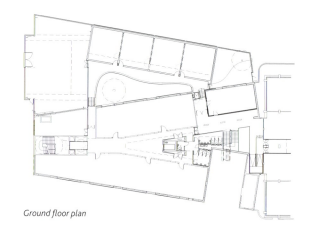
Ground floor plan

The new teaching block provides a mix of flexible teaching spaces and purpose-built facilities arranged around an internal atrium and an external courtyard. Specialist areas, including a new televison studio, post-production facilities for the Media School, and a bank of interconnecting photographic studios, are housed in the single-storey Oswin Street wing. The main teaching block, comprising two 7.5-metre-deep converging floor plates, is naturally ventilated and incorporates external louvres, exposed concrete soffits and automated windows.

The new 'street' includes a triple-height glazed entrance, a roof-lit circulation space at ground and first floor level, a new ground floor lecture theatre and links to all existing buildings. The 'street' is defined by a 76-metre-long roof plane that extends out to the existing square to mark the entrance.

▲ *Metal louvres shade the interior of the atrium in the new teaching block.*
▶ *The new internal street and connection with the existing building.*

JOHN MAKEPEACE WORKSHOP

Beaminster, Dorset
2001

Set in the Beaminster conservation area, the site of the proposed workshop is adjacent to the mature gardens of a restored eighteenth-century manor house. The brief was to provide new spaces for the design and crafting of unique pieces of furniture.

The barn-like building can be read in a number of ways. On the one hand, it is a straightforward, utilitarian, timber building, subordinate within the picturesque composition of the main house, garden and outbuildings. However, the scheme is also intended to express its role as a creative design studio, and this is reflected in the robust, sculptural form that encloses light and airy volumes in contrast to the darker spaces of the manor house.

A single enveloping roof wraps the studio. The ridge and eaves of the roof run at different angles, the latter falling on the entrance side to a single exaggerated downpipe. The timber-clad walls describe the plan's irregular shape and incorporate different-sized windows. An informal stair leads from the entrance to the upper studio, which is dominated by a large north-lit window at the furthest end. At this point the internal volume is allowed to puncture the roof of the upper studio, providing a panoramic view over the landscape.

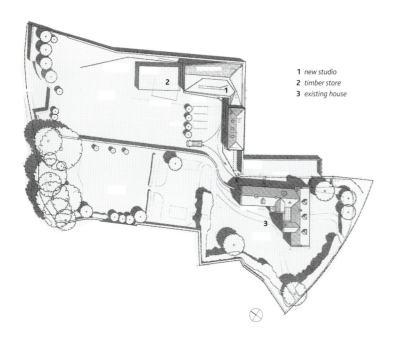

1 new studio
2 timber store
3 existing house

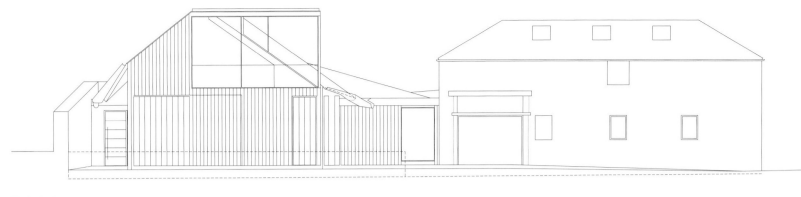

North elevation

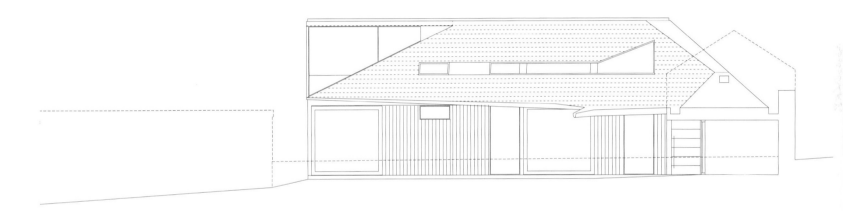

West elevation

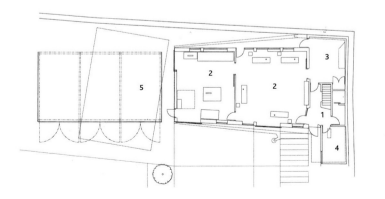

Ground floor plan

First floor plan

1 entrance lobby
2 workshop
3 finishing
4 store
5 timber store
6 office
7 studio
8 gyp room

QUEEN'S HOUSE
Greenwich
1999–2002

Completed in 1617 by Inigo Jones following his grand tour of Italy, the Queen's House is regarded as the first Palladian-style building in Britain. The subsequent development of Wren's Greenwich Hospital made Jones' masterpiece the axial focus of Greenwich Park. Managed in recent years by the National Maritime Museum, the Queen's House suffered from the lack of a clear visitor entrance, poor circulation routes and disabled provision. A new step-free entrance, reception space, picture lift and stair were required to allow the building to be used as a gallery.

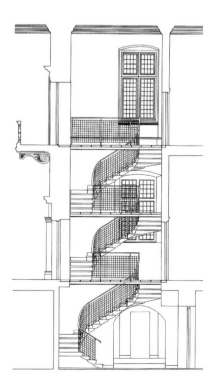

The most viable location for a new visitor entrance was the original central door to the basement, aligned on the central axis between the 'horseshoe' stairs facing the river. The external ground level was reduced and a dished, semicircular forecourt was laid to establish a suitable formality. This clarification of access enabled the ticket desk, cloakroom, toilets and shop to be regrouped in the newly rendered vaults of the basement, apart from the significant historic rooms above.

From the basement level, a new lift and cantilevered stair provide a coherent visitor route to all levels of the building. This new stair is located symmetrically opposite Jones' original Tulip Stair and revisits both the formality and structural daring of his design. The woven metal balustrade and continuous bronze handrail rework the materials and making of its seventeenth-century precedent.

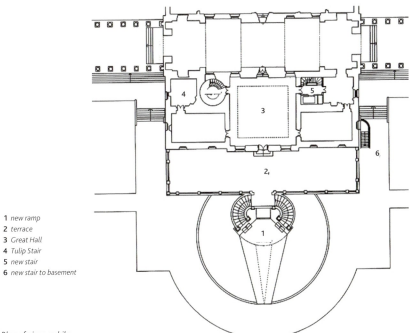

1 *new ramp*
2 *terrace*
3 *Great Hall*
4 *Tulip Stair*
5 *new stair*
6 *new stair to basement*

Plan of piano nobile

Appendices

Chronology
1983–2003

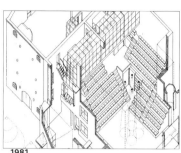

1981
Reading Enterprise: Malthouse
Conversion of brewery to an arts centre

1983–90
The Mound, Edinburgh
Public square
Open competition, 1st place
p20

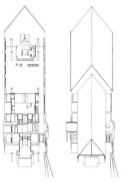

1985
Rosyth Church
Invited competition

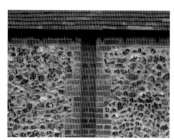

1986
Manor Farm, Farningham, Kent
Village housing

1987
Hollybank, Chorleywood, Hertfordshire
Restoration/extension of CFA Voysey house

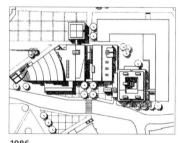

1986
Aston Triangle, Birmingham
Open competition, 2nd place
p24

1987–90
Clove Building, London
Conversion of warehouse to office and retail
p26

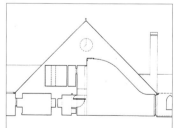

1987
Felsted School, Essex
Dining Hall
Invited competition, 2nd place
p30

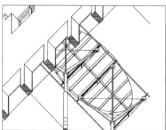

1987
Sainsbury's Supermarket
Open international ideas competition, 1st place
p32

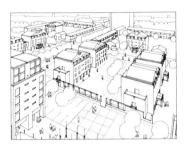

1988
Royal Victoria Docks, London
Housing

1988
Cross Ness, Thamesmead
Housing
Invited competition, 1st place

1988
British Ambassador's Residence, Moscow
Diplomatic residence
Invited competition, 2nd place

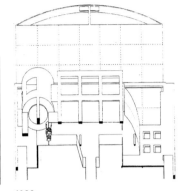

1988
Canary Wharf, London
Office building

1988
Emerson Valley, Milton Keynes
Village housing

1989
Brown House, Amersham, Buckinghamshire
Private house

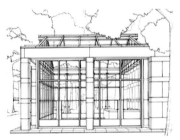

1989
Hyde Park Pavilion, London
CEGB Vent shaft and cafe
Invited competition

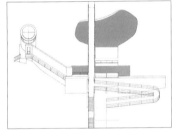

1989
Penguin Enclosure, Edinburgh Zoo
Civic building
Open competition

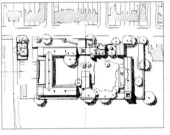

1989
Christ Church, Corpus Christi, Oxford
Student housing
Invited competition, 2nd place

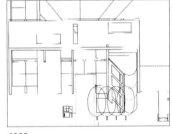

1989
Commonwealth Institute, London
Major additions
Invited competition, 2nd place

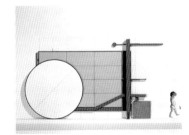

1990
British Museum Forecourt, London
'Rediscovering the public realm', Heinz Gallery
p34

1988–90
Centrepoint windshelf, London
Public space and refurbishment of office tower
p36

1990
Minories, London
Office building
p38

1990
Dulwich Picture Gallery, London
Open competition, 2nd place
p40

1990
Ashland Place, London
Office building

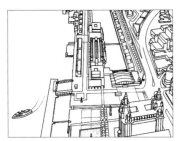

1990
Princes Dock, Liverpool
Masterplan
Invited competition

1988–91
Scott Howard Building, London
New showroom and offices
p44

1991
Whitechapel, London
Office building

1991
University of Essex, Colchester
Extension to library
Invited competition, 1st place
p46

1991
Fitzwilliam College, Cambridge
Student housing
Invited competition

1991
Science Park, Oxford
Car park

1992
Oak Yard, Blackheath, London
Private house
p50

1992
Stephen Bull's Bistro and Bar, London
Restaurant
p54

1992
Bishopsgate, Spitalfields, London
Office building

1992
Whitbybird offices, London
Office refurbishment

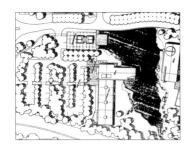

1992
Penrhyndeudraeth, Wales
Business park, open competition, 2nd place

1992
Arts Centre: Loughborough, Leicestershire
Cultural building, open competition

1992
Garrick Street, London
Urban housing and retail

1992
Crossrail Hanover Square, London
Underground station

1992
Ashland Place, London
Conversion to office building

1990–92
33-35 Blandford Street, London
Urban housing and retail
p58

1993
New London House, London
Refurbishment of 12-storey office tower

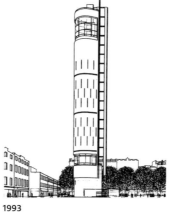

1993
Glasgow Tower, St Enoch's Square
Observation tower
Open competition, 3rd place

1993
National Museum of Contemporary Art, Helsinki, Finland
Open competition, 4th place
p62

1993
Thames Footbridge
Open competition

1994
People's Palace, Royal Festival Hall, London
Restaurant and bar in grade-one listed interior
p66

1994
Hayward Gallery, London
Temporary pavilion
p70

1994
Royal Festival Hall, London
Temporary education workshop
p70

1994–2003
South Bank Centre, London
Masterplan
Invited competition, 2nd place
p72

1994
Dollar Bay, London
Urban housing
Invited competition, 2nd place

1991–95
Sarum Hall School, London
Girls preparatory school
p76

1990–95
Pierhead, Liverpool
Public landscape
Invited competition, 1st place
p82

1992–95
British Embassy, Dublin
New embassy building
Invited competition, 1st place
p86

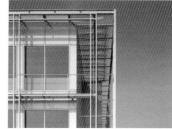

1993–95
Nunnery Square, Sheffield
Office building and business park
p94

1993–95
Rosalind Franklin Building, Cambridge
Student housing, Newnham College
Invited competition, 1st place
p98

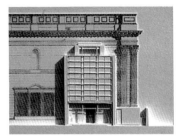

1995
Fitzwilliam Museum, Cambridge
Extension to existing building
Invited competition

1995
US Navy, London
Entrance lobby

1993
Botolph Lane, London
Office building

1994
Sheffield City Centre
Urban regeneration masterplan

1995
Derby Road, Watford
Office building

1993–95
Students' Union
University of Southampton
Extension
p106

1995
Inhabited Bridge, River Thames, London
Bridging the City proposal,
Royal Academy, London

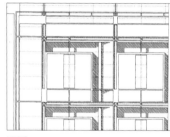

1995
British Embassy, Berlin
Invited competition

1995
Regent Street, London
Masterplan for redevelopment
Invited competition, 1st place
p108

1995
Glasgow Housing
Open competition

1995
FC Brown Showroom, London
Furniture showroom

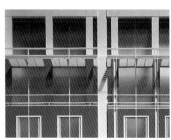

1995
18-19 Hanover Square, London
Crossrail over-site development

1995–96
Contemporary Applied Arts, London
Craft gallery and shop
p110

1994–97
Abbey Mills Pumping Station
Industrial building
Invited competition, 1st place
p114

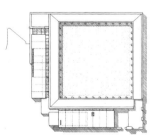

1996
Norwich Cathedral visitor centre
Invited competition, 2nd place

1996
Performing Arts Centre, Bristol
Invited competition

1996
Thames Marker, Richmond, Surrey
Visitor centre
Invited competition

1996
Coalhill, Edinburgh
Housing
Open competition

1997
The Hague, Netherlands
Office building
Invited competition, 1st place

1996
2 Brindleyplace, Birmingham
Office building

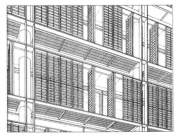
1997
Science and Engineering Library, University of Edinburgh
Open competition

1997
Waltham Cross Bus Station
New bus station

1995–97
No 1 Prince of Wales Road, London
Conversion to housing
p122

1996–97
Goldsmiths College, University of London
Rutherford Information Services Building
p128

1996–2001
The Place, London
Contemporary dance studio
p134

1997
23–25 Soho Square, London
Office building refurbishment

1998
Royal Institute of British Architects, London
Bookshop

1998
Civic Centre Hackney, London
Technology and learning centre
Open competition

1998
Greenwich town centre, London
New DLR station
Open competition

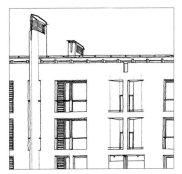
1998
Jesus College, Cambridge
Student housing
Open competition

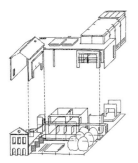

1999
Limavady, Ireland
Arts centre
Open competition 1st place

1999
Queen Mary Westfield College, London
Laboratories
Open competition

1997–2001
Tate Britain, London
New entrance and landscaping
p138

1997–2002
Horniman Museum, London
Refurbishment and extension
p142

1997–2002
Horniman Museum Conservation Building, London
p148

1997–2001
South Hill Park Arts Centre, Bracknell
Invited competition, 1st place
p150

1997–2003
The Hospital, London
Performance space, studio and club
p154

2000
58-62 Newman Street, London
Office refurbishment

2002
Castlehaven Road, London
Housing development

2000
Ericsson Headquarters, London
Office building
with Gert Wingårdh Architects

1996–2003
St Martin's Court, Paternoster Square, London
Office building   p156

2001
Arnold House School, London
New entrance and school accommodation

2000
Royal Institute of British Architects, London
House architect, council chamber

2001
Abbey Orchard Street, London
Office refurbishment

1997–2000
Holden House, London
Listed building conversion for office/retail
p158

1997–99
Blackburn House, London
Private house
p160

1998–2001
Blackwell, Cumbria
New museum in grade-one listed house
p164

1997–2000
6 Brindleyplace, Birmingham
Office building
p168

1999–2000
Scotch Malt Whisky Society, London
Private members room
p170

1999–2001
Cowdray Park, West Sussex
Golf course and clubhouse
Invited competition, 1st place
p172

2001
Piccadilly, London
Office building

2002
QAS, London
Conversion of industrial building to office headquarters

1999–2002
Fulham Broadway, London
Facade to retail development
p174

1999–2002
Milton Keynes College, Bletchley
New campus
p178

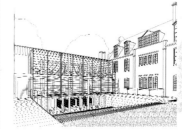

1999
Newnham College Library
Extension to existing library
Invited competition
p182

1999–2002
The Guardian Newsroom, London
Archive and visitor centre
p184

1999–2003
One Piccadilly Gardens, Manchester
Mixed-use development
p188

1998–2003
London College of Communications
Refurbishment and extension
p192

2001
John Makepeace Furniture, Dorset
Workshop and offices
p196

1999–2002
Queen's House, Greenwich, London
Reorganisation of access to Inigo Jones' building
p198

Bibliography

General works

Order, Orthodoxy and the Orders
Bob Allies
Architectural Review, vol. 173, no 1036, 1983 June, p59-65

Six young architects
Colin Amery
RIBA Transactions, vol 3, no 1, 1984, p52-56

Past sympathies
Dan Cruickshank
Architects' Journal, vol 185, no 4, 1987 Jan 28, p14-17
[Hollybank, Chorleywood]

Winning ways
Mark Swenarton
Building Design, no 872, 1988 Feb 12, p18-23

Profile – Young practices: Bob Allies and Graham Morrison
Martin Spring
Building, vol 254, no 7611 (33), 1989 Aug 18, p24-25

Urbaner Dialog
Leonardo, 1990 Oct/Nov 6, p34

Kolme rakennusta [Three buildings]
Chris Bearman and Meri Makipentti
Arkkitehti, vol 89, no 7/8, 1992, p84-91
[Scott Howard, Stephen Bull's Bistro and Bar, Ashland Place, London]

Shelled and cored
Architecture Today, no 28, 1992 May, p44-45
[Ashland Place, London]

Royal Festival Hall, Sir Leslie Martin and Associates [Architecture in Detail]
John McKean
Phaidon Press, 1993

The art of process: architectural design in practice
Louise Rogers
RIBA, London: 1993, p71

Turn of the Century
John Welsh
Building Design, no 1107, 1993 Jan 15, p1, 12-13
[Joint third prize Glasgow Tower]

Stripping back to the frame
Marcus Field and others
Architects' Journal, vol 198, no 21, 1993 Dec 1, p29-39
[New London House]

Contemporary British architects: recent projects from the Architectural Room of the Royal Academy Summer Exhibition
Peter Murray and Robert Maxwell
Prestel, 1994

Architeckturpreise in England
Jochen Wittmann
Deutsche Bauzeitschrift, 1994 Feb 2, p18-19

Housing and Office Development in London
Detail, vol 34, no 5, 1994 Oct/Nov, p602-605

Allies and Morrison
Architects' Journal, vol 202, no 20, 1995 Nov, p38-41
[A look at some of the firm's recent and future projects: Rosalind Franklin Building, Newnham College, Cambridge, p38; Students' Union Shop, University of Southampton, p39; Pierhead, Liverpool, p39; Morrison House, p39; Renovation, Royal Festival Hall, p40; Office building, Botolph Lane, City of London, pp40-41; Office building, Derby Road, Watford, pp40-41; Office building and Crossrail station, Hanover Square, London, pp40-41]

Allies and Morrison
Edited by Annette LeCuyer
University of Michigan College of Architecture & Urban Planning and Allies and Morrison, 1996

1997 Building Awards
Jessica Cargill Thompson
Building, vol 262, no 7985 (14) Supplement, 1996 Apr 11, p3-57

Blooming business, hard landscaping
Will Callaghan
RIBA Journal, vol 104, no 3, 1997 Mar, p81, 83, 85
[Allies and Morrison and BDP projects]

Allies and Morrison
Rowan Moore
Architecture and Urbanism, A+U, no 9 (324), 1997 Sept, p56-117
[Morrison house, Blackheath, p62-65; Stephen Bull's Bistro & Bar, p66-69; Sarum Hall School, London, p70-75; Pierhead, Liverpool, p76-79; British Embassy, Dublin, p80-87; Nunnery Square, Sheffield, p88-91; Rosalind Franklin Building, Newnham College, Cambridge, p92-99; Student Union Shop, University of Southampton, p100-103; Regent Street, London, p104-107; Bristol Centre for the Performing Arts, p108-111; Abbey Mills Pumping Station, p112-117]

Space: the final affront
Louise Rogers
Building Design, no 1330, 1997 Nov 21, p8
[RIBA Bookshop]

True to type
Margaret Richardson
RIBA Journal, vol 104, no 12, interiors supplement, 1997 Dec, p12-15
[RIBA Bookshop]

Un'architettura attenta [Assiduous architecture]
PG Raman
Spazio e Societa, vol. 20, no 81, 1998 Jan/Mar, p52-67
[Contemporary Applied Arts, London, p53-54; South Bank projects, p55-57; Blandford Street, London, p58-61; Sarum Hall School, London, p62-64; British Embassy, Dublin, p65-67]

Interview: Allies and Morrison
Stanley Collyer
Competitions, vol 9, no 3, 1999, p26

Modernist hall that broke all the rules
Giles Worsley
Daily Telegraph, Arts & Books, 1999 May 1, p7
[Royal Festival Hall refurbishment]

Musical reprise
Isabel Allen
Architects' Journal, vol 209, no 23, 1999 June 10, p59-63
[Royal Festival Hall refurbishment]

On the crest of a new wave
Nonie Niesewand
The Independent, 2000 Apr 9, p19
[Southbank]

Special issue. Buro & Architektur [Offices and architecture]
Julia Triphaus
Deutsche Bauzeitschrift, vol 48, no 10 supplement, 2000 Oct, p42-45
[Ericsson headquarters in London]

Not just a pretty face
Kester Rattenbury
Building Design, no 1507, 2001 Oct 26, p14-15
[Fitzwilliam College Gatehouse]

New London Architecture
Kenneth Powell
Merrell Publishers, 2002 Jan, p82-85
[Paternoster Square, Arsenal Football Club redevelopment, Royal Festival Hall refurbishment, The Place]

The Mound

The Mound competition
Prospect, no 18, Summer 1983, p i-iv

Space on the Mound
Architects' Journal, vol 178, no 34/35, 1983
Aug 24/31, p20-23

Winners picked for piazza at Edinburgh Mound
Ian Latham
Building Design, no 654, 1983 Aug 19/26, p24

Public space, Edinburgh
Architectural Review, vol 175, no 1043, 1984
Jan, p25

Sense of the civic
Brian Edwards
Building Design, no 944, 1989 July 7, p20-21

The Clove Building

Working with Old Buildings
Dan Cruickshank
Architectural Review, vol 183, no 1094, 1988
April p83-84

Working places: problems and opportunities
Peter Davey and others
Architectural Review, vol 189, no 1129, 1991
Mar, p27-78

Essence of clove
Clare Melhuish
Building Design, no 1029, 1991 Apr 5,
p20-23

Sainsbury's Supermarket Ideas competition

Ideas for a Supermarket
Architectural Review, vol 181, no 1084, 1987
June, p75-86

British Museum Forecourt

*Rediscovering the public realm:
an exhibition at the Heinz Gallery*
Deyan Sudjic and Peter Murray
Blueprint, no 66, 1990 April, p51-54

Dulwich Picture Gallery

New pavilion at Dulwich
Clive Aslet
Country Life, 1990 Sept 13, p178-179

Soane success
Clare Melhuish
Building Design, no 1003, 1990 Sept 14,
p13-16

Modernism and Soane
Dan Cruikshank
Architects' Journal, vol 192, no 12, 1990
Sept 19, p26-33

Scott Howard Building

Allies and Morrison: the pleasure of abstraction
Martin Richardson
Architecture Today, no 18, 1991 May,
p40-42, 45-46

Furniture showrooms in London
Bauwelt, vol 83, no. 42, 1992 Nov 6, p2383

En trompe-l'oeil: la galerie Scott Howard
Techniques & Architecture, no 412, 1994
Feb/Mar, p116-117

Oak Yard

Modern house
John Welsh
Phaidon Press, 1995

*Choosing the best of today: Christopher
Bradley-Hole chooses the Morrison house,
Blackheath*
Michael Hall and Jeremy Musson
Country Life, vol 191, no 43, 1997 Oct 23, p69

Stephen Bull's Restaurant

Modern Cuisine
David Redhead
Blueprint, no 88, 1992 June, p30-31

Palate's palette
Liz Clare
Designers' Journal, no 79, 1992 July/Aug, p36-39

Bull's Smithfield Bistro
Carl Gardner
RIBA Journal, vol 99, no 11, 1992 Nov

Hotels et restaurants
Florence Michel
Architecture Interieure Cree, no 251, 1992
Nov/Dec, p114-115

Admiral Court

A question of balance
Clare Melhuish
Building Design, no 952, 1989 Sept 8, p10

Detail
Architecture Today, no 15, 1991 Feb,
p78-79

Tectonic reality – Sleight of hand
Colin Davies
Architectural Review, vol 191, no 1149, 1992
Nov, p64-67

*Sanierung, Erganzung, Umnutzung
[Refurbishment, rehabilitation]*
Roland Jesse
Detail, vol 34, no 5, 1994 Oct/Nov, p602-605

Hayward Gallery Pavilion

Extending the Hayward
Deborah Singmaster
Architects' Journal, vol 200, no 19, 1994
Nov 17, p9

Besondere Orte [Special places]
Sabine Schneider
Baumeister, vol 92, no 3, 1995 Mar, p17-19

People's Palace, Royal Festival Hall

Palace coup
Penny McGuire
Architectural Review, vol 198, no 1183, 1995
Sept, p27-31

Interieur: Les Bars
Beatrice Loyer
Techniques & Architecture, no 425, 1996
April/May, p102-103

Return of the People's Palace
Rob Gregory
Building Design, no 1485, 2001 May, p40-41

Sarum Hall School

Class distinction
Clare Melhuish
Building Design, no 1052, 1991 Oct 11, p18

Layers of meaning: Sarum Hall School
Anthony McIntyre
Architecture Today, no 61, 1995 Sept, p36-41

British Embassy, Dublin

The making of Allies in Dublin
Architects' Journal, vol 193, no 17, 1991
April 24, p9-10

August opening for embassy
Building, vol 260, no 7895 (22), 1995
June 2, p11

New British Embassy, Dublin
John E O'Reilly, Irish Architect, no 111, 1995
Oct, p28-34

Modern Manners
Demetrios Matheou
Architects' Journal, vol 202, no. 20, 1995 Nov,
p28-29

A diplomatic solution
David Pennington and Shane de Blacam
Architects' Journal, vol 202, no 20, 1995 Nov
23, p43-52

Work studies: An Irish solution
Penny McGuire
Architectural Review, vol 199, no 1190, 1996
April, p34-39

Made in our own image
Colin Amery
Perspectives on Architecture, no 29, 1997
June/July, p48-53

Special report: Embassies
Jane C Loeffler
World Architecture, vol 63, 1998 Feb,
p82-105

Nunnery Square

Park Life
John Welsh
RIBA Journal, vol 102, no 6, 1995 June, p38-45

Students' Union Shop, Southampton University

Shop assistance
Naomi Stungo
RIBA Journal, vol 103, no 5, 1996 May, p42-47

Contemporary Applied Arts

The craft of gallery design
Marcus Field
Architects' Journal, vol 203, no 7, 1996 Feb 22, p26-27

From black hole to brave new world
Amicia de Moubray
Country Life, vol 190, no 24, 1996 June 13, p118-119

Abbey Mills Pumping Station

Pumping up the volume in East London
Deborah Singmaster
Architects' Journal, vol. 202, no 1, 1995 July 6, p26-27

The romance of sewage disposal
Robert Bevan
Building Design, no 1302, 1997 Apr 4, p8

Pump and circumstance: Architects of superstructure
Martin Spring
Building, vol 262, no 7985 (14), 1997 April 11, p42-45

Sewage Works
Roderic Bunn
Building Services, vol 19, no 7, 1997 July, p40-41

Excremental vision
Marcus Field
Blueprint, no 142, 1997 Sept, p34-36

Young English duo explores the importance of being modest
Brian Carter
Architectural Record, vol 186, no 2, 1998 Feb, p29

Die ungeliebten Orte – Zweckbauten fur Stadthygiene und Sicherheit
[Unloved places – functional buildings for public health and safety]
Olaf Winkler
Baumeister, vol 95, no 3, 1998 Mar, p17-53, 93-96

De l'architecture industrielle, a l'architecture souterraine, EOLE
[From industrial to subterranean architecture, the EOLE]
Anne-Laure Egg
Architecture Interieure Cree, vol 288, 1999, p56-57

Prince of Wales Road

Open House: Allies and Morrison in North London
Stephen Bates
Architecture Today, no 111, 2000 Sept, p36-49

Rutherford Information Services Building

Modern renaissance
Simon Pepper
Architecture Today, no 88, 1998 May, p34-40

Concurso del Goldsmiths College en Londres
Pasajes, Arquitectura y critica, no 42, 2002 Dec, p6

The Place

New id on the block
Lia Hattersley
Blueprint, no 182, 2001 April, p46-49

Leading the dance
Penny McGuire
Architectural Review, vol 209, no 1252, 2001 June, p82-85

Recent projects: London College of Printing, The Place
Architecture and Urbanism, A+U, vol 370, 2001 July, p110-116

A sense of Place
Kenneth Powell
Architects' Journal, vol 214, no 14, 2001 Oct 18, p32-41

Tate Britain Landscape

Tate Modernised
Martin Spring
Building, vol 266, no 8205 (41), 2001 Oct 12, p20-21

Tate a tete
Amanda Birch
Building Design, no 1508, 2001 Nov 2, p13-15

New approach
Penny McGuire
Architectural Review, vol 212, no 1266, 2002 Aug, p28-29

New public landscaping at Tate Britain
Architecture and Urbanism, A+U, no 10 (385), 2002 Oct, p8-12

Horniman Museum

Eclectic selection
Kester Rattenbury
Building Design, no 1538, 2002 June 21, p12-15

What's new pussycat?
Peter Lewis
Museums Journal, vol 102, no 7, 2002 July, p40

Joined-up thinking
Blueprint, no 197, 2002 July, p26

Space and identity: Townsend transfused
Penny McGuire
Architectural Review, vol 212, no 1265, 2002 July, p64-69

Michael Horniman Conservation Building

Collector's piece
Robert Bevan
Building Design, no 1450, 2000 July 21, p14, 19-20

South Hill Park Arts Centre

Theoretical Practice: Allies and Morrison at South Hill Park
Martin Pearce
Architecture Today, no 133, 2002 Nov, p20-30

The Hospital

The Hospital
Architecture Today Handbook, 2005 Jan, p14-15

Holden House

Foyer pleasure
Kieran Long
Interiors for Architects & Designers, 2001 Jan/Feb, p30-32

St Martin's Court, Paternoster Square

Squaring up
Kenneth Powell
Architects' Journal, vol 218, no 16, 2003 Oct 30, p28-45

House in Holland Park

Interiors studies
Vicky Richardson
RIBA Journal, vol 107, no 3 Interiors Supplement, 2000 Mar, p16-20

Housing as homes: Layers of Meaning
Mark Swenarton
Architecture Today, no 118, 2001 May, p44-55

Blackwell

Bright future for the Arts and Crafts?
Andrew Mead
Architects' Journal, vol 208, no 9, 1998 Sept 10, p56

Home is where the art is
Dean Hawkes and Diane Haigh
Architects' Journal, vol 214, no 3, 2001 July 19, p26-35

Blackwell revisited
Alison Forrest
Prospect Scotland, no 91, 2003 May/June, p34-35

6 Brindleyplace

City of Today: Birmingham's Brindleyplace
Ian Latham
Architecture Today, no 71, 1996 Sept, p26-36

West Midlands
Nancy Cavill
Building, vol 264, no 8078 (10), 1999 Mar 12, p43

Pret a port-air
Andrew Pearson
Building, vol 265, no 8121 (4), 2000 Jan 28, p48-51

Datafile: Project Review
Martin Spring
Building, vol 266, no 8180 (15), 2001 Apr 12, p62-67

A formal number
George Demetri
Brick Bulletin, 2001 Winter, p12-13

Scotch Malt Whisky Society

Interiors
Martin Spring
Building, vol 265, no 8132 (15), 2000 Apr 14, p54-73

Cowdray Park Golf Club

Allies and Morrison wins the open
David Taylor
Architects' Journal, vol 210, no 6, 1999 Aug 12/19, p16-17

Fulham Broadway

Deyan Sudjic
Observer Review, 2003 Dec 14

The Guardian and Observer Archive

Celebrating all our yesterdays
Alan Rusbridger
The Guardian, 2002 June 8, p8

Read all about it
Tom Dyckhoff
Guardian Weekend, 2002 June 15, p42-46

News storeys
Barrie Evans
Architects' Journal, vol 216, no 11, 2002 Sept 26, p36-38

One Piccadilly Gardens

Seven-storey slab completes Manchester's urban oasis
Martin Spring
Building Magazine, 2004 Apr 22, p16

City lights – an office building completes a public square in the heart of Manchester
Architecture Today, no 151, 2004 Sept, p87-93

London College of Communication

Recent projects: London College of Printing and The Place
Architecture and Urbanism, A+U, vol 370, 2001 July, p110-116

Peace Makers
Hugh Strange
Building Design, no 1604, 2003 Nov 28, p11-14

Queen's House

Fit for a Queen
Penny McGuire
Architectural Review, vol 211, no 1259, 2002 Jan, p 74-77

Credits

Photographs
Peter Cook: Frontispiece, 8B+MB, 10B, 12, 22-25, 40BC+BR, 41, 46-47, 49-53, 54T, 55-57, 63-64, 79R, 80-91, 93-97, 99, 101-103, 106-110, 115-117, 134L, 135, 136L, BR+MR, 137-143, 153T+BL, 154L, 155, 164, 165R, 171-173, 194-196, 198BL, 200TCL, ML, MCL, MC+BR, 201TL, TCL, ML, BCL, BC, BCR+BR, 202TCL, ML, BL, BC+BCR, 203TR, BL+BCL, 204TC+TCR, 205TC, MC+BR
Simo Rista: 9T + M
Jim Scrivens: 9B
Antonio Martinelli: 11
Lothian Regional Council: 19, 198TC
Chris Edgecombe: 33, 48T, 200MCR
Dennis Gilbert/VIEW: 65, 98, 100, 121, 123-133, 144-151, 156-159, 174-177, 180-181, 182 B, 183-186, 187BL+R, 189-191, 203MC, MCR+MR, 204TR, ML, MCL, MCR+MR, 205TL, MCL, MCR, BL, BCL+BC, Charlotte Wood: 66-67, 72-77, 163, 199LM, 200MR, 201MCL, MC+BL, 204 MC+BCL, 205TCL
Studioworks/Eamonn O'Mahony: 68, 201MCR
Robert Cameron: 69R, 104T
Andrew Putler: 104B, 111, 114, 154R, 169-170, 199BL, 202MCL, MCR+BCL, 203TL, 204TCL+BR, 205TR
Etienne Clément: 118-119
Nicholas Kane: 152, 153BR, 204BL+BC
Nick Wood: 160-162
Chris Tubbs Photography: 166-167, 205TCR
Paul Smoothy: 182T
David Millington Photography: 187TL
Hélène Binet: 204BCR
Allies and Morrison: all other photographs

Models
Kandor: 33, 37, 68, 114, 154R, 170, 199BCL+BCR, 201CCR, 202BCL, 203TL, 204BR
Network: 104B, 174L, 202MCR
Allies and Morrison: all other models

Others
Courtesy of Artek, Helsinki. Project carried out with Bearman Makipentti, Helsinki: 30TCR
Museum of London, Gavin Morgan Picture Gallery: 40BL

Every effort has been made to acknowledge the source of photographs and illustrations; we apologise for any errors or omissions. Image locations abbreviated as L = left, R = right, M = middle vertically, B = bottom, T = top, C = centre horizontally

Exhibitions

1984
Six Young Architects
RIBA Heinz Gallery, London

1985
40 under 40
RIBA Gallery, London
The Mound, Edinburgh

1987
40 Under 40
RIBA Gallery, London
Sainsburys

Royal Academy Summer Exhibition, London
Hollybank, Chorleywood; Aston University Centre, Birmingham; RIBA Gallery extension, London

1988
Royal Fine Arts Commission for Scotland Exhibition, Edinburgh
The Mound, Edinburgh

Royal Academy Summer Exhibition, London
Sainsburys; Brushfield Street, Spitalfields, London

1989
Rediscovering the Public Realm
RIBA Heinz Gallery, London
British Museum Forecourt

Royal Academy Summer Exhibition, London
HM Ambassador's Residence, Moscow; Admiral Court, London

1990
Salon International de l'architecture, Paris
The Clove Building, London

Royal Academy Summer Exhibition, London
Christ Church, Corpus Christi, Oxford

1991
Royal Academy Summer Exhibition, London
Three City office buildings, London; Dulwich Picture Gallery, London

1992
Royal Academy Summer Exhibition, London
Sarum Hall School, London; British Embassy, Dublin

University of Manchester School of Architecture
Recent projects

City Changes
Architecture Foundation, London
Spitalfields, Building A, London

1993
Art of the Process, RIBA Gallery, London
Morrison House, London

Royal Academy Summer Exhibition, London
CEGB Hyde Park Pavilions, Thames Footbridge competition

City Changes
Barcelona, San Paolo, Prague
Spitalfields, Building A, London

1994
New British Architecture
Architectural Institute of Japan, Tokyo
Recent projects

1995
Allies and Morrison Retrospective
Matthew Architecture Gallery, Edinburgh
Recent projects

1996
Venice Biennale
University of Edinburgh Science and Engineering Library, Royal Academy Bridging the City

Bridging the City
Royal Academy, London
Inhabited Bridge

Allies and Morrison Retrospective
US schools of architecture (1996-98)
Recent projects 1986-1998
Wolk Gallery, Massachusetts Institute of Technology

New Urban Environments
Japan (1996-97)
British Embassy, Dublin

1997
New Works/Future Visions
Sao Paolo (1997-98)
Selected projects

1999
4th Bienal Internacional de Arquitectura
Sao Paolo
Bristol Centre for the Performing Arts

Allies and Morrison Retrospective
Helsinki, Finland and Delft, Holland
Recent projects 1986-1998

Allies and Morrison
1983–2002

Bob Allies	Benny O'Looney	Cecilia Dubois	Julie Humphryes	Mark Reimer	David Abergel
Graham Morrison	Hatice Arabaci	Vicky Thornton	Martin Eglin	Mammad Tabatabai	Francesco Draisci
Tim Makower	Hugh Strange	David Bonta	Alex Wraight	Morna McKay	Graham Simpson
Paul Appleton	Simon Williams-Gunn	Ruth Selig	Mandy McInnes	Shona Fox	Jonathan Schwinge
Joanna Bacon	Sarah Fussell	Stuart King	Nicholas Champkins	Sian Bowser	Dave Stanley
Stephen Ryan	Penny Gardiner	Rawden Pettitt	Rodrigo Brito	Anna Poetsch	Debra Penn
Michael Taylor	Ian Carson	Tommy Chung	Adam Parkyn	Alistair Twiname	Nichola Schroeder
Ian Hill	Glen Millar	Hendrik Heyns	Ashley Munday	Anne Milbank	Gail Stott
David Amarasekera	Gavin Harris	Natalie Black	James Parkin	Helen Berry	Andrew Dowding
Robert Maxwell	Adrian Morrow	Thom Gill	Jason Syrett	Jan Kuzminski	Julia Chambers
Deborah Miller	Ioana Sandi	Tat-Sing Tey	Jenny Lovell	Liz King	David Stanley
John Pardey	Joe Witchell	Barry Steadman	Nicholas Hornig	Mark Simpson	Mark Robinson
Joanna Weddell	Wendy Boyd	Alistair Cook	Robert Nisbet	Mike West	Abel Law
Philippe Faure	Graham Vicary	James Fraser	Karen Fugle	Ruth Treacher	Umberto Emoli
Josephine Saunders	Liz Parr	John Barber	Nigel Reading	Chantelle LaRose	Aoife Keigher
Ron Yee	Ria Summerhayes	Nina Quesnel	Annie Templeton	Erin Reynolds	Patrick McLeod
Robert Wood	Sundeep Bharma	Robin Gray	Andrew Dean	Katerina Mathouidaki	Emma Wiren
Martin Markcrow	Tina Bird	Simon Pendal	Oli Heywood	Lawrie Robertson	Sophie Blunden
Chris Bearman	Harriet Bagnall	Melanie Monteith	Robert Yates	Rob Gregory	Sarah Lyne
Robert Payne	Megan Williams	Edward Watson	Karen Swords	Saskia Vandersee	Andre Rodrigues
Sian Jones	George Stowell	Christina Johnsson	Sophie Vickers	Simon May	Rikki Kuittinen
Neil Campbell	Mary Ackom	Fiona Szabo	Jaime Sanson-Chirinos	Thomas Koppelmann	Emma Jones
Pauline Stockmans	Emma Wiseman	Isobel Whitelegg	Eamon Broderick	Charlotte Hagg	Victoria Baynes
Louise Clayton	Helena Thomas	Gabor Gallov	Nadja Sugden	Hina Farooqi	Billy Choi
Sheila Hammond	Thomas Reinke	Lien Lu Sin	Lynn Taylor	Jason Cully	Amanda Heagren
Ian Sutherland	Di Haigh	Oliver Ralphs	Stella Kamba	Julia Haselmayer	Myrlin Toone
Annette Lecuyer	Andrew Green	Sarah Beatty	Finbarr Finn	Lola Sheppard	Mirei Yoshida
Alison Licsik	Michel Cant	Adrian Lee	Simon French	Richard Myers	Ben Flatman
Mark Pearson	Sharni Joel	Bryan Storm	Dionysis Zacharias	Eric Yeung	Yvonne Lea
Paul Summerlin	Graham Perring	Sheila Corbett	Michelle Miller	Corinna Simon	Denis Olette
Marianne Davys	Jonathan Hendry	Sky Grove	Alex Marcoulides	Donald Matheson	Leyra Villoria
Grainne Crooks	Gordon Shrigley	Rebecca Huggins	Camilla Wilkinson	Genna Ryder	Richard White
Deborah Bookman	Jill Annarino	Sarah Simmon	Lucy Sharrock	Michael Durran	Jim Rooney
Kevin Sugden	Malcolm Cormack	Catherine Garbi	Miranda Reynolds	Nick Peri	Anthony Martin
Philip Toms	David Wagner	Lorraine Wan	Liz Nettleship	Robert Park	Kirsten Church
Lucy Britton	Yee Lee	Aaron Fletcher	Michelle Stott	Susan McLean	Oxana Krause
Timothy Godsmark	Anna Bardos	Lisa Donnell	Robin Williams	Zeya Win	Lianne Peterkin
Kathleen Morrison	Eddie Taylor	Pat Seymour	Terence Seah	Marco Gelsomini	Lucia Pflucker
Honor Thompson	Steve Taylor	Kasia Boguslawska	Ian Patterson	Henry Chown	Young-in Oh
George Novakovic	Stephanie Eberle	Robin Walker	Lisa Webb	Bärbel Gamm	Oliver Cooke
Mark Way	Julia Davies	Toby Birtwistle	Neil Shaughnessy	Ernest Tsui	Angela Wharton
Kate Fitchie	Indu Ramaswamy	Adrian Fowler	Peter Besley	Paula Craft	Peter Clarson
Laurie Hallows	Wicek Sosna	Jeremy Leman	Rupert Fisher	Greg Holme	Ewan Morrison
Miranda Doyle	Jane Parker	Emma Huckett	Suzanna Heape	Eric Martin	Daniel Prinz
Chris Evans	Beatrice King	Helen Logan	Joanna Rippon	Jaqueline Milmo	Jonathon Broughton
Diana Periton	Clare Roberts	Frank Amankwah	Mark Taylor	Jake Noble	Kirsty Yaldron
Chris Proctor	Martin Bradley	Joanne Clark	Michela Ruffatti	Julian Coward	Matthew Cochrane
Salla-Johanna Laurikka	Amy Harris	Miranda Webster	Miles Leigh	Liz Marley	Amy Lam
Susan Sears-Carter	Suzie Lloyd	Steve Larkin	Mark Camillin	Marianne Voswinkel	Amy Ewing
Michael Greville	Sophie Bradford	Melissa Barker	Ajay Khana	Oliver Houchell	Drusilla Powell
Stephen Archer	Catherine Harrington	Iona Foster	Matt Davis	Matthew Stares	Helen Sparks
Cathy Milligan	Simon Fraser	John Morgan	Karen Wong	Neil Dusheiko	Charlotte Barrows
Julian Cowie	Gemma Collins	Jonathan Coote	Ricardo Gandolfi	Yves Racine	Susannah Shaw
Sarah Jackson	Duncan Thomas	Keith Evans	Adam Smit	Sue Potter	Goksen Kolcak
Kevin Allsop	Barnaby Hewitt	Laura Stephenson	Chris Butler	Miles Wilkinson	
Terence J McCarthy	Ben Elsdon	Christopher Cribb	Mark Gilder	Andreia Lima